ARE YOU R
W

"To wake up your angelic nature and to experience help from the angels read this compellingly insightful book."

Mark Victor Hansen, co-author #1 Bestseller,
Chicken Soup for the Soul

"Spirituality is an imporant dimension in healing. This book share with you an honest realization that may also transform your life."

Dr. Fred Hui, M.D., Past President,
Acupuncture Foundation of Canada

ALSO BY
ANGELICA EBERLE WAGNER

Are You Ready for a Miracle?
. . . with Angels

A Practical Guide to Understanding
Angels in Everyday Life

By Angelica Eberle Wagner

Are You Ready for a Miracle?
. . . with Angels

A Practical Guide to Understanding
Angels in Everyday Life

By Angelica Eberle Wagner

Dreamakers International Inc.

Canadian Cataloguing in Publication Data

Wagner, Angelica, 1952-
    Are you ready for a miracle?

ISBN 1-896375-00-6

1. Self-actualization (Psychology).   I. Title

BF503.W33 1997   158.1   C97-931985-7

First Printing May 1997

Cover and interior book design/art production:
Karen Petherick, Petherick & Associates, Markham, Ontario,
Division of BIA Communications Limited

Printed and bound in Canada by
Webcom Limited

Dedication

To my beloved in heaven:
Mentor, Guardian, Wisdom

To my beloved on earth:
Soul-mate, Playmate, Best Friend

To my earthly cherubs:
Jennifer, Andrea, Jake and Lauren

My heartfelt thanks to:

My family
Karl, Andrea and Nicholas Zeeb,
Brigitte and Joachim von Schwerin

My editor
Murray Fisher

My staff
Gerard C. Meyers
Gay Richardson

Friends of "Are You Ready For A Miracle?":
Anthony Robbins, James Redfield, Leland Val Van De Wall,
Mark Victor Hansen, Jack Canfield, Thomas T. Tierney,
Elizabeth C. Tierney, Dave Liniger, Gail Liniger, Dr. Jay
Holder, Dr. Rachel Holder, Dr. John De Martini,
Athena Starwoman, Gay Richardson, Marianne Drew,
Stu and Carole Munro and
The Canadian Chiropractic Forum

I am deeply grateful to all the people throughout the world
that have shared their miracle stories and experiences with
me in the writing and creation of this book. I especially
encourage and advise the healers to continue their work
with joy and love. The great goodness that they create
transforms the universe. They are cherished. They are
needed. . .continue to live with great purpose.

Dear One,

I have written this book just for you. My wish is that you may come to know the magnificence of your own creation. Whatever is hurting your body or soul, understand that it can be healed. You have been created perfectly in the image and likeness of God. You can release the shackles of whatever infirmity binds you or has bound you.

Today is an instant in your life. You need only to ask for the healing, and you will receive it. Learn to seek the miracles of your birthright, as intended in the creation and through the angels.

The release of the creative life force energy within you will lead you to greatness. You need nothing more. You are enough. You are complete. The Great Creator brought you to this time and place to accomplish great and urgent work. Get up, get on with it, do it now! You are important. I believe in you.

Understand that you are never alone. The angels in their glory were created for you lest you stumble on the smallest stone. Understand above all else how very much you are loved. Appreciate the divinity in your soul.

If this book saves only one of you from pain or alters the course of your life, through the transformation of your own innate power, it will have been worthwhile in the effect of its energy. The greatness and goodness that lies buried within you needs only to be released one moment at a time for the greatness and goodness of all mankind.

Today is the first day of the rest of your life. Live it well. Energy and time are the blessings of a glorious inheritance. The transformation of the universe lies within your grasp now. Because of the gift and contribution of YOU, the world is better.

Remember, YOU are the miracle!

Angelica

Table of Contents:

Table of Contents:

Introduction

ARE YOU READY FOR A MIRACLE? WITH ANGELS.

*W*hen you begin to look for the
extraordinary in your daily life, you
begin to see that miracles occur not
only in the Bible, but in nature's lessons of
wonder every day. The power of every ocean
and every star can inspire and create mighty
miracles in your life. I have collected the stories
of healing angels in order to honor life and honor
the healing professions. These stories are a series
of miracles; all true, all factual, that caused a life
change for those who experienced them. The
miracles have inspired, given purpose and
direction, and caused such changes that the
people they touched were never the same
physically or emotionally again. They have been
transformed—from human form to earthly
divine human form.

These stories are a tribute to the angels who
have changed my own life. Each of the miracles
in this book was a gift from God. The miracles
were sent to bring peace, joy and good will in
the same purpose the angels were sent to
intercede. The angels are the intercessory agents
from heaven showing us a different way of
responding to a circumstance that we believe in
our human experience to be limiting. It is the
purpose of this book to make angels real in your
life as they have been in mine. This is a practical
guide to understanding angels in every day life,

and using the opportunities that they bring to you to create miracles daily. It is a practical guide to using the tragedies that show up in your life as transformational springboards of finding your divine self.

One of the greatest healers that ever lived was born with the fanfare of stars and wise men. Not all angels, healers or miracle makers arrive in that way. Although the beginning of documented human miracles began then, there have been many examples of the unexplained, of miracle occurrences, of angel visitations, of synchronicity of events that go beyond our comprehension of the possibilities of nature, into the realms of the extraordinary, the impossible, the miracle realms. It is those realms that this book explores, to bring them closer to you, to bring them into reality wherever you are today and whatever you believe today.

When I was very little, my mother gave me a picture of an angel watching over a brother and sister as they crossed a turbulent bridge on a dark and stormy night. I always believed that angel was one of my guardian angels sent to watch over me. It was not until many years later on a dark, stormy night while driving with a friend of mine, that I came to know the reality of my own angels.

I had a sudden strong feeling that there was something wrong in the direction that we were driving. Had I followed my intuition, we would have stopped the car and driven down another street immediately.

Suddenly, from nowhere, another car drove

through a stop sign right at us. When we came
to a stop after the jarring crash his car had
crashed on top of ours. The blow was shattering
for all of us. On impact, my seat belt
disconnected and my head went straight up into
the roof as I was the passenger. I didn't know
then that this incident would change my life
forever.

For the first 24 hours, I was sent to
emergency for observation, X-rays, and drugs to
control the pain. They sent me home afterward.
There were no obvious injuries. I just felt
stiffness in my neck, shoulders, and a pain down
my right leg. I was told to take drugs for the
reduction of spasm, or to control any pain.
Twenty-four hours later however, I was
paralyzed from the waist down, and spent the
next six weeks in a wheelchair. All I craved to
do was to walk again. That's all! I didn't care
how. I just wanted to walk.

As a real estate agent at that time, I was
supporting my young family of four children on
my own. After six weeks of inactivity and no
income, I became alarmed that I'd never
improve! I finally worked up the courage to ask
the medical doctor what his opinion was of my
progress. His answer, "There was no obvious sign
of permanent damage, but the fact that you
could not walk after six weeks of medication,
therapy and rest made it obvious that you
probably would not walk for a long time—if
ever." Although the situation was not hopeless, I
chose to believe it was hopeless.

To this day I have not forgotten the terror of

feeling trapped in a body that was "in-valid", not being able to do all the fun things I enjoyed doing, especially with my children. After crying oceans of tears, I finally decided to ask my mother who knew about healing because of her own challenges with health. She told me to see a chiropractor. I had nothing left to lose, and everything possible to gain, so I went.

Within three adjustments I moved my right leg – just a little – actually inches. From that point forward I knew I would walk again. Six weeks later, I actually stood up. I haven't stopped running since.

The results of those next six weeks were the inspiration that caused me to write this book. Ordinary people still don't know about the miracles in natural healing. Ordinary people still don't know the power of angels that show up as healers in every day life. Angels appear in many disguises whenever we need them to minister to our smallest concerns. We just need to recognize them, invite them in, and give them permission to do their angel magic.

I came to know my angels were real not through triumph, but through disaster, through pain not through pleasure. I began to experience real joy when I called angels into my life daily. Miracles began to happen in spite of me and my belief of "that's impossible" getting in the way. When I started to look for circumstances where angels showed up to help and heal my life in ordinary ways, their intercession intertwined as a part of all the relationships in my life.

In healing there are daily miracles. Healers

in the broadest sense are the integrators of the spirit, mind and the body. There is in natural healing no real cause for change except as an intervention of God—the God factor showing up. Healers give the miracle an opportunity to show up by freeing the body from interference. When the body is free of interference, it heals itself.

As I expanded this thinking to life and its challenging situations, I began to understand how removing interference through angel interventions also healed the soul. Rather than using life as a repository or bank for inactivity or for blame about what didn't happen, we use life and the situations of despair to commit to something. As we lose the past, explore the depth of love, we grow the potential for divinity in our humanity.

There is no such thing as an undercover healer or an undercover angel. Both healing and angel interventions expose themselves. Our help in making miracles manifest sooner is to talk about them frequently. The more we take the time to talk about the miracles, the more often the miracles will show up. This changes our destiny as a society.

Because of my own healing and the impact that had in my life, I have written a series of books exploring true victories of hope over despair, triumph over tragedy, wellness over disease. In almost all cases the victim of the tragedy had nothing left to lose. The only answer facing them had been despair, in some cases death. Many victims of tragedy or disease were degenerative cases left to die or disintegrate in pain. This series of books will give hope in the innate power of miracles to those who read them. You only need to ask and the "earth angels" will help you, too.

Unless there is an extraordinary reason we do not usually recognize miracles. If we did, we would begin to see them as they were intended to be, signposts of the future, signposts of power, signposts of the innate creativity of the inner spirit of the soul unfolding butterfly-like in harmony with the magnificence and majesty of the universe. Exploring with our helpmates on earth, our earth angels, creates resilience in our life, expands our humanity and unmasks our own courage. Angels give hope, comfort and solace to the future of our divine creativity by releasing the power of our immortal soul.

Frequency in miracles occur from a call to the spirit. When events shifted and my responses to them shifted, life changed more dramatically than I could ever have imagined. There seemed to be a force greater, truer, clearer, that was and is in charge. I knew the universe was unfolding as it should. As I listened, followed and believed the force of the good things in the universe, my life was transformed, magically, almost instantly.

This book tells stories of angel interferences that transform lives. How are miracles transforming your life?

Will you let them?

Prologue

*I*n Islamic beliefs, it is not only one man who makes the perfect and total ascension, but all humans who have attained a state of perfection. Is a state of perfection possible today? Do we believe in perfectionism as the only way of life? In every age man has had its "axis" for being the perfect knower or lover of God. The perfect man is the one who repeats this ascension and actualizes God's central position in the cosmos here on earth. The perfect man raises his standards.

We are in a space and time in the universe where we realize our own "Raphael" of healing, of our own inner being. Raphael was the archangel responsible for healing. When man realizes his own responsibility and potentiality for transcendence, he will discover also that he has control of his universe both internal and external, from the cellular level to the universal level and from the microcosm to the macrocosm.

Thus choosing to hear the call of knowledge and of nature brings about our own "Raphael" experience. Our world then becomes a place of benevolence rather than malevolence, of compassion and conviction, rather than injustice and apathy. Angels act as the practical instruments that bring joy back to human life.

How are angels connected with the human body? Since we were created by God, we are already complete. Somehow we don't feel complete. God sends His angels to take care of us in ways we could never expect to make our lives more joyful.

The human body serves as an object of contemplation as man was being made in the image of God and is, therefore, most worthy of being loved; most worthy of being perfect in every way; most worthy of healing in order to achieve this divine perfection. Angels are the messengers of this perfection and are sent by God to lead us to this perfection.

The greatest of all the messengers between heaven and earth is the Angel of Love himself. This archangel presides over destiny, over the soul, over our own angels. The union of the soul with God through the angelic beloved, the guardian angel, wakes us up to our destiny.

Tension created by the destructive forces of evil awaken mankind to the possibilities of his soul. Both the tensions and the tragedies that we experience are placed there to awaken us to our own greatness. These tensions are deliberately placed in our paths to show us the light. Without the tensions and life experiences, the gift of light remains an illusion. The tensions and tragedies that we don't want are exactly the seeds of change that we need.

These are not just esoteric words. The light of the universe is found in each person who goes beyond and through whatever tragedy has been set in his life in order to create and illuminate his divinity. This divinity is within each of us. The tragedies are placed there, not to crush our spirit, but to illuminate our power.

Light can always be found in these losses; whether this is personal, financial, health, or relationship loss. Therefore, darkness, pain or depression are meant to bring us closer to our courageous spirit. The lessons of pain are meant to bring us further from the fall of the Angels from Ego into humility, from suffering to bliss, unity, divinity, and transformation. When tragedies come into your life, these are exactly the areas that open your heart to receive miracles. Acceptance of the miracle then has the magical quality of power. You have the power within you to conquer anything! Accept power.

These very tragedies plunge you into the spiritual world and lightbeam you through a portal of faith so when you need help, you simply perceive the problem in a different way, learning to call the angels into your life to guide you. The tragedy does not need to be accepted as the final conclusion to the way your life is supposed to be. Angels are the practical answers to creating the miracles you need in your life and opening your heart to find your own life spirit that you lost in the tragedy.

This concept is so simple, most people fail to perceive it, to wake up to it.

Think of yourself as an incandescent power, illuminated and perhaps forever talked to by God and his messangers.

Brenda Ueland ~

xxi

Part One

Introduction to Angels

WHAT ARE ANGELS?

*A*ngels are messengers of hope or warning. They are ministering spirits or agents of change sent to alter your current thinking. Generally, they arrive in human form as small children or ordinary people dressed in the garb of the culture. We don't think of them as **Earth Angels**, but they are.

Angels also arrive as an ***intuition***, a sudden knowledge or connection that is made instantly and unexpectedly on a deep heart level after days, weeks or months of searching or fruitless labour. These intuitions are characterized by a feeling of truth or absolute certainty of the correct decision or action to be taken as a result of the intuition. They are also accompanied by a feeling of being in the correct space and time in order to accomplish the work that needs to be done. There is a feeling of deep connectedness

1

with nature, energy and the innate power of creativity.

The presence of the angels is revealed in a sense of physical, emotional, and psychological connection to the belief in healing. C. G. Jung, a famous psychological healer, stated that every patient who fell mentally ill had lost the sight of that which the living religions teach: a sense of emotional healing and a deep fulfilling sense of being loved.

Reward is brought by angels to those who are faithful to their ultimate purpose as it is unfolded in their lives. We are each ultimately called to create God's great purpose in ourselves. It becomes a meaningful purpose in our lives when we choose to listen to the message. Until we choose to listen to that message, we continue to experience pain. Pain being the great leveler in life, you choose to deal with it or let it stop you where you are.

Angels are pure intellect. They are dwellers in the holy temple of the body. They are also pure in spirit, and can travel without effort to aid those who are ill. Illness means being separated from your own wholeness.

Angels were created in order to communicate the occurrences of earth back to heaven. They were created to be the gossips of God. They are the intermediaries between heaven and earth and exist as agents to the divine. Being on the divine scrolls, they have a job to do on earth. It's up to us to call on their services.

Angels may show up in different disguises,

but their message is always one of love. Even the message from the angel of death is a message of love for those who are left behind to carry on. If we start to live our lives more in a state of love, the obstacles, barriers, pain and tragedies will be dismissed. They get the message that love prevails here and quickly leave.

Angel Lore

A NATURAL HISTORY OF ANGELS

According to Western civilization and thought, it is assumed that only Christian and Judaic belief represents the existence of angels. But, contrary to such thought, angels have appeared in art, philosophy, shamanistic visions, Hinduism and Buddhism. What do all these beliefs have in common?

It is an understanding that angels are sent by God as His messengers. They are the inhabitants of the intermediate world. As spiritual beings, they possess qualities which are more enhanced than human powers. In the Bible angels perform the will of God as intercessory agents between heaven and earth. They hover over the humans to fulfill the tasks for which humans were created, which is to know God. Then they fly back to the heavenly realm to report and repeat what they have seen on earth, usually to bestow blessings on the humans. Everything that is good occurs with the intervention of the angels. Mohammed went so far as to say that every raindrop is the manifestation of an angel's wish.

The Greeks coined the word, "angelos" to describe messengers, then later this phrase became the messengers of the Gods. In the Bible, the translated word "angel" appears almost three hundred times from Genesis to Revelations as a specific type of being. A declaration by the council of Nicea in 325 B.C. declared the belief in angels to be an official dogma of the church. This was the doctrine of coinherence to formulate the divination of the body and the soul.

Even in 325 B.C. the current thought was to bring the body and the soul together through the intercession of the angels. This new dogma was so far ahead of its time that it must have unloosed angel worship because less than twenty years later another council denounced it as idol worship.

Finally, in 787 A.D. the Seventh Ecumenical Council established a limited dogma of the archangels together with their names and special purposes, and this took firm root in Eastern belief. Angels, then constituted the relationship between the world and God. As far back as 787 A.D., angels were believed to be real and a part of society.

THE ORIGIN OF ANGELS

Where did angels come from? How did they get here? According to the Book of Enoch in Judaic tradition, 2 Enoch 29:3-4

"From the rock I cut off a great fire, and from the fire, I created the armies of the bodiless ones, ten myriad of angels, and all the armies of the stars, and the cherubim and seraphim, and the ophanim, and all these from the fire I cut out."

It leads the reader to believe that the angels were created from light and fire. Is it any wonder that angels show up again, whenever the elements of light and fire come into our lives? The original manuscripts to the book of Enoch were found in Ethiopia and later translated. This book was written in the second century B.C. In more than one religion or belief, angels occupied a common place.

In the Bible in Genesis 1:6 it says: "And God said 'Let there be a firmament in the midst of the waters.' And God called the firmament HEAVEN. And the morning and the evening were the second day."

The firmament and heaven were believed to be the places where the angels dwelt. These were created before the inhabitants of earth. Imagine the presence of angels before the existence of any other form, other than God? Angels have been around to help us for a very long time. So why haven't they shown up before to explain their purposes to us?

1 Enoch 40 states; "I saw a hundred thousand times a hundred thousand, ten million times ten million, an innumerable and uncountable multitude, who stand before the glory of the Lord of Spirits encircling that house."

Michael, Raphael, Gabriel, Phanuel and the numerous other holy angels that are above. "The Antecedent of Time came with a hundred times a thousand and ten million times a hundred thousand, angels that are countless. Together with you shall be there dwelling places, and together with you shall be their portion. They shall not be separated from you forever and ever."

Thus long before man was created, the angels were created as direct companions and helpmates to mankind; to walk with, to share with, and to experience earthly events together. It was a divine partnership.

The promise of the heavens was that you shall not be alone.

Imagine how powerful this promise was. That within each of us is the dwelling place of our divine soul and our angelic perfection. Before man was created, there was a plan to have a permanent bridge to divinity. One within the soul of man and one linked through the spirit of the angels sent to take care of us forever. Our link to God is completely inseparable, beyond time into eternity. Angels are the physical manifestation of God's word. They show up every day in many ways.

Angels were glorified in art by poets,

painters and theologians, acknowledged in literature and in the foundation of Christianity. Over the centuries angels were depicted and sculpted as works of art for devotional or sacramental purposes. In many instances the angels were shown as ordinary beings rather than possessing wings. They had the capability to fly, to communicate without speaking and other extraordinary powers.

Because there are millions of angels, there are enough for each of us to have at least one. I like to think that I have many angels, each one shows up in my worst disasters. They know that I need them. Each is his own message, in his own manner, to comfort me and give me strength in a way that I could not possibly have done on my own.

THE NATURE OF ANGELS

No matter how close to God the angels may be, they still share the status of creatures in humanity. As truly spiritual creatures, they are totally free from human limitations. They have no bodies therefore they never die. They have the ability to fly, to pass through space and time without effort. The physical appearance of angels in biblical encounters varies. It is questioned whether angels eat or ever have sex. Bodily functions are not of great importance to angels.

In the New Testament when angels appeared at a time of high glory, such as the birth of Jesus, they arrived in a blaze of light, themselves illuminating and enhancing the event by their glorious appearance. At the time of His death an angel that had the appearance "like lightning and a raiment as white as snow" (Matt 28:3) came to roll away the stone of his tomb. I think that's what fools us, today, we expect all this commotion to accompany angel visitations, rather than finding angels showing up as ordinary people who have messages that could guide us and change our lives. I find it becomes a matter of angel recognition, rather than lack of angel visitation.

Angels belong to a uniquely different dimension of order than we humans. They come complete with a higher knowledge, an inner knowing of what to do and when to do it. They appear to aid and advise the humans and give messages. Indeed they frequently "are" the message. Angels appeared many times to people to announce the good news (Jgs:13:3), to warn in time of danger (Gn 19:15), to guard us from evil forces, to teach us, to nourish and protect us.

In the Old Testament, the Angel of the Lord possesses a spiritual nature and also assumes a voice and a vision. Other theologians insisted that the incorporeality of Angels did not rule out being created of some subtle matter so that they are bodiless but numerical. Being numerical means that they can be counted. Being subtle means they accomplish their work in indirect ways or means. Because there are so many angels there are enough for each of us to have several to take care of us. The scriptures refer to angels

9

as a succession of powers in diverse places in time. Not only can we have several angel helpers, but they can show up for different reasons in places in our lives where we need help.

APPEARANCES OF ANGELS

Angels often appear in human form. In earlier times biblical encounters showed them as ordinary people. Isn't it amazing that we fail to recognize these powers in human beings? An "earth angel" is an angel that comes in the disguise of a human in order to help us when we are in a state of despair. Earth angels know precisely when to show up. They appear at the exact moments that they are needed to help humans.

Imagine the immensity of this notion that we might have several angels to call upon in order to accomplish our great work and purpose in the universe. These angels would not always be "magical beings of light" carrying wings, but always emanating goodness, kindness, generosity, mercy and concern in helping us accomplish some great task that we feel unempowered to do on our own. It is the concept of being human that requires exploration here. In being human we arrive with bodies as well as minds, hearts and spirits. Are angels sent when we forget about those parts of ourselves that we neglect?

Have you thought about the "earth angels" that have arrived to help you through a really tough time? Have you been an earth angel to help someone else? Did someone show up almost miraculously at a time when help was important to you?

HOW DO YOU EXPERIENCE YOUR ANGELS?

1. Is there a sudden strong intuition or feeling that you cannot ignore?
2. Is there either a subtle or a dramatic sign that there will be a change or a shift in circumstance? Has something especially good happened unexpectedly that has changed your way of thinking?
3. Is there a resignation of your own will to a circumstance, yet a belief that "only good things will follow" from this point forward.

Yesterday is a cancelled check.
Tomorrow is a promissory note.
The only cash that we have is Today.
Spend it well.
Leave the past in the past.

4. Watch the sequences of events that follow. You may be surprised.

HOW DO YOU RECOGNIZE YOUR ANGELS?

1. Have you ever experienced buckets of tears or raucous laughter for no reason at all? What happened before or after the event? Do you know why you cried or laughed? What did you do next?

When an inner situation is not made conscious, it appears on the outside as fate.

C. G. Jung~

11

2. Has someone said something that made the hair on your arms stand up? Or have you experienced shivers or goose bumps? Was there a feeling of complete truth in the statements that were made?

3. Has someone you did not know very well solved a huge problem for you with little or no effort?

4. What tragic sequences in your life created a wonderful result in the end? Did you need the tragedy to realize the appearance of angels in your life ?

5. Has someone shown up in your life to illuminate your innate power in a way you were not expecting? How did it happen?

6. Who has come into your life to help you in a way you have not understood before? Do you believe you were touched by an angel?

Is there any way you can share
this angel visitation with others?
Talk to me about it, call:
USA 1 (800) 861-8707 Ext.6226
Canada 1 (800) 927-8139 Ext 6226

Part Two

Functions of Angels

THE GUARDIAN ANGEL

Everywhere I researched the writing of this text, the miracles of love permeated the very fibre of the research. It seemed to become clear that the greater the catastrophe that had occurred, the greater the capacity for the miracles of love to appear. Generally the miracle was accompanied by the appearance of angelic forces who showed up before the miracles, or in the events that happened in synchronicity to miracles. In every instance, the antecedent to amazing miracles was preceded by catastrophe in one form or another. Almost as though an invisible force "had gone before" to make room for the miracle to occur. If you are sensitive to this power, you can change any disaster in your life into a point of power and courage.

In the middle of difficulty lies opportunity.

Albert Einstein~

13

I've come to believe that angels take guardianship over us only with our permission, and the more often we call on them for help the more often they show up to help us. This is particularly true of the guardian angel.

When man opens his heart, even for an instant, the insight and intuition he receives comes from his guardian angel.

When he finally hears the call to the spiritual life, the subtle substance of his inner being acts out for him the drama of his inner life. It is in the subtleties that transformation occurs from humanity to divinity. It is the guardian angel who sometimes brings circumstances into our lives that can be viewed as tragic at the time. These circumstances are intended to become the stepping stones to greatness. The guardian angel knows when to take man to divinity and it's usually not an easy path.

The guardian angel knows you and loves you best. He is your inner self, your conscience, your most joyful self. He is the angel that brings about your happiest moments. He is the angel that creates peacefulness in all situations and circumstances. Peacefulness being the essence of divine love.

The Persian philosopher, Avicenna, speaking of the guardian angel said that the soul must grasp "the beauty of the object that it loves". The guardian angel loves, cherishes and sees beauty in you. That is why it is so important to follow his inner direction, even if you really don't agree with him. Human souls are drawn to their guardian angel as to their "Beloved". In

Though we travel the world to find the beautiful, we must carry it within us, find it or not.

Ralph W. Emerson~

14

learning to love and obey the guardian angel, we move to a higher level of spirituality .

It is also believed by mystics and prophets, who trained their active imagination to transform through the power of love, that a human being is made into an angel. I don't dispute the theory. My guardian angel is Val, someone I loved very much who has finished his earthly work and now takes care of me from heaven. He speaks to my higher self. I call on him for guidance. I don't always like or appreciate the messages, but he is usually correct in his assessment of the issues.

This beloved is also called the Witness, because his beauty bears witness to God's Beauty, and through this angel, one might witness the reality of all truth. One comes to know truth through the prompting of the guardian angel. When you are finally ready to listen, justice comes.

The guardian angel creates desire for greatness within us. Desire causes motion on the level of the spheres. Literally, it brings people events into our lives, sometimes in commotion, in order to create change. The guardian angel pushes us out of our comfort zones often into uncomfortable circumstances to create change in our lives. Although the guardian angel is the most protective of all the angels, he will allow you to learn your own lessons if you choose not to obey his voice. As you are afflicted, he will also be afflicted in order to save you from yourself. Isaiah says, "The angel of His presence saved him, in his love and pity."

In order to live a creative life, we must lose our fear of being wrong.

Joseph Pearce~

15

We can always count on our guardian angel to have pity and compassion. The guardian angel has the perception of the big picture of your life and continues to give you the lessons that you need until you see the big picture, too. My guardian angel kept me alive through that accident so I could find my purpose. It was my guardian angel who brought circumstances into my life that changed my destiny.

In a broader sense, there have also been "earth angels" in history that have acted as guardians to humanity. By their actions and the love that they had for humanity, great works were accomplished. Although there were many human angels that created change for society, I remember most vividly the philosophers Plato and Socrates, the geniuses Copernicus, Einstein, Newton and Darwin, the industrial revolutionists, Bell, Edison and Ford.

Although they were all guided by an inner force and an inner vision of greatness, they contributed to society and to history in such a way that made their own lives immortal. They stood beside society at a time when it was ready for change and continued to listen to their own inner guardian, although they were publicly perceived as being strange or rather weird.

These earth angels had attained such height of spiritual clarity that in continuing to live with their purpose, they brought goodness and fullness to the world and the world could never forget them. Weren't all these people acting as guardians to a society that had not caught up to their genius? Weren't all these mortals acting in

There is a vitality, a life force energy, a quickening that translates into action, and because there is only one of you in all of time and history, this expression is truly unique.

Martha Graham~

an angelic way that was foreign to humans, but natural to their own state of immortality created by their guardian angel. The guardian angel gives each of us the outer courage and inward fortitude to follow our dream.

In angel lore, it is believed that one of the gifts that God bestowed upon the angels was eternal life. I don't believe that just angels or even guardian angels have eternal life. I do believe that humans, who listen to their inner voice and contribute to the changes of greatness in the world will, always be remembered and honored through time and space into eternity. They are the guardian angels of society and create human immortality.

HOW DO YOU KNOW YOU HAVE A GUARDIAN ANGEL?

1. Have ordinary people with an extraordinary message or vision come into your life? What did they ask you to do?
2. Has a catastrophe become evident? How bad was it? Could you have died from it? Why didn't you?
3. What have you learned from this tragedy?
4. Have you felt the presence of a power greater than yourself urging you to accomplish some great work. Are you doing it? Why? Why not? If not now . . . when?
5. Has someone that died sent you a message or gift?

I am with you and will watch over you wherever you go. I will not leave you until I have done what I promised you.

Genesis 28:15~

17

6. Did you meet someone who spoke to you in unusual short commands? What did they ask you to do ?
7. Did you express gratitude or joy to this person?
8. What happened next?
9. If you removed your greatest obstacle to live your greatest dream, what would happen to your life?

*Wendy Luke is an inmate unjustly accused of the murder of her own child. She is serving the second year of a 20-year term. The District Attorney has recently agreed that there is evidence of her proof of innocence, as told by her mother Kathleen Byers. She believes her guardian angel will rescue her from an unjust sentence.**

GUARDIAN ANGEL

Last night I had a dream
It had a tale to tell,
I dreamed I saw an angel
Poor thing, he wasn't well.

His body bruised and battered
His wings were ripped and torn;
This angel could hardly walk;
He looked so tired and worn.

I walked right up to him,
"Angel? How can this be?"
He turned around and paused a bit . . .
Then spoke these words to me

"I'm your guardian angel.
A great task as you can see.
You've run amok all your life,
Look what it's done to me.

These bruises are from shielding you.
In time, both dire and ill.
Those dangerous drugs you've used.
I've often paid the bill.

You see my wings are ripped and torn.
A noble badge I wore.
How often they have flown you
From the evils and the horror."

Each mark is it's own story
Of deadly wounds destroyed,
You've made me wish more than once
that I was unemployed!
If only you could make it on your own. . .
Oh, don't' fret or worry, you'll not be left alone.

– Contributed by Kathleen Byers
– Poem by her daughter Wendy Luke*

19

The first story is about a courageous woman who found her angels when she experienced tragedy in her life. The angels showed her a different way to respond to a situation that she found hopeless.

An Angel In My Kitchen

It is difficult for me to know where to begin my story. This has been a long road with many twists and turns.

I was 30 years old and the mother of a very beautiful, very healthy and active eighteen-month-old boy. I had a job that I thoroughly enjoyed and a husband who was loving, caring and supportive. I had all the basics of a good and happy life. When I look back on that time, seven years ago, I remember feeling that my life could not have been better. I was, like most people, blissfully flowing along in the denial of our common fate; a denial which was somehow essential to my peace of mind. I never thought about mortality in a serious way. Little did I know that my reality was about to change—almost as abruptly as if I had crashed into a brick wall while travelling at 90 miles an hour.

I remember fighting with my doctor because I wanted a mammogram. She hesitated, saying, "Thirty-year-olds never get breast cancer." I, however, knew in my heart that something was terribly wrong. After all, it was my body, so I persisted until the doctor reluctantly agreed to send me for the test. That was the first time in my life I stood up and asserted myself. And did I receive reinforcement for this lesson: I was diagnosed with breast cancer. I had a modified radical mastectomy, and 15 of 22 lymph nodes removed from under my arm showed malignancy.

By the time my husband and I left the doctor's office we were in total despair. I had never felt so alone or so abandoned. I was sure nothing good would come of this. I was convinced I would soon be dead. We began our drive home in silence, punctuated only by the sounds of our sobs.

Suddenly, the energy in the car seemed to change. My husband began to speak as if he were guided to do so, saying that we would fight. Other people have beaten cancer, he pointed out, and we, too, would do whatever was necessary to beat it together. Fortunately my fatalistic attitude was short-lived thanks to the strength of my husband and family. Although at the time I was sure it was my husband who was going to save me, I now know that, through my own strength, hope, will and faith, I saved myself.

I refused to allow this cancer to run my life. I had a family to care for, a child to raise, and a life to live. From that moment on we began an all-out war. We set out to educate ourselves on the different options available, both mainstream Western and so-called "alternative" approaches. We would only see doctors and other health professionals who dealt with us in an open, informative and caring way. We always insisted on knowing exactly what was going on and why so we could make informed decision.

Through all this, we called everyone we knew to solicit support and prayers. Friends and family flocked to our side. It's amazing how people respond when another is in need. I learned much about the innate goodness of people. I learned how essential sharing love is to the human experience. I began to feel the love in my heart and the hope which ultimately sustained me through this journey. The possibility of miracles and the wonder of life became everyday thoughts to me. I began to questions my thought patterns more. This, I found, was an important factor in my well-being. I pondered why I thought it more realistic to expect a negative outcome and came to the realization that it was no more realistic than to expect a positive one. I opted to expect the positive.

I began to seek more out of life. I have always asked my God to show me the right path and to provide me with the tools I need. I have had much chemotherapy and even a bone marrow transplant. These things were all gifts from God. I wanted more, however, and that drive is what led me to seek the aid of a healer.

I have always been interested in the mysteries of healing and I began to pursue this. One morning, by chance, I saw Los Angeles based Dr. Eric Scott Pearl and some of his patients on a TV talk show. I believe the

topic was alternative healing. I was struck by his
gentleness and humility. He has truly been given
the gift of healing. He doesn't know why he was
chosen or where the gift came from. "Call it
God, Love or Universe," he says, yet somehow a
healing power works through him. His patients
receive healing which were otherwise unheard of
in today's world.

When I first met Dr. Pearl I was weak from
chemotherapy. Not only did I require a
wheelchair to travel from place to place, the rest
of the time I was confined to my bed. I had
spent seven weeks in the hospital in isolation
while doctors tried to figure out how to treat my
blood count which, for the previous two
months, had dropped dangerously low and
seemed insistent upon remaining there. The only
thing they knew for certain during those seven
weeks was that I required blood transfusions
every other day in order to survive. To add insult
to injury, I was also suffering from shingles. I was
determined to leave the hospital in time for my
first appointed healing session—and I did just
that. My healing began the day my husband and
son checked me out of the hospital and wheeled
me in to see Dr. Pearl. From then on, things
have become miraculously better.

As Dr. Pearl ran his hands a few inches
above my body, I could feel warmth. I saw many
bright colors, a white star, and an exquisite
white light. I also saw an intensely beautiful
violet light, a violet hue I had never seen before.
I felt the sensation of invisible hands touching
me in a healing way. I realized the presence of

23

loving, joyful beings. It felt as if angels were having a party all around me. Not being a person who regularly sees angels, this was a very significant event for me. I wanted to get up and join in the fun. I felt my heart open in an intense surge with every emotion imaginable. It was an enchantingly beautiful experience. The only other time in my life that I can remember feeling this way was when I gave birth to my son.

All too shortly, I heard the gentle voice of a female angel gently saying, "You're done." Just then, Dr. Pearl brought me out of the session as if he had heard the angel, too. These loving angels came to me again in our next two sessions (I had three sessions, one a day for three days, and each was a beautiful as the one before). Without words, the angels gave me peace, love, joy, playfulness and hope, all things I needed in my life. During my sessions with Dr. Pearl, these angels allowed me to feel what I can only describe as the energy of my life—it was like the buzz or hum of my being.

The angels stayed with me for several months; we visited daily. They illuminated my path, helping me to see my needs more clearly and to become the healthy, vibrant person I am today. They came to me in dreams and while I was awake. Sometimes I would see them and other times I would sense them. They always gave me the answers I needed. I am eternally grateful for this gift.

The angels don't reveal themselves to me anymore, although I'm sure they continue their watch. I used to know when I was about to see the angels because, the most heavenly scent of vanilla ice cream cones would fill the air, as if to announce their arrival. I no longer see them, there is no more vanilla ice cream scent. That day I walked into my kitchen and was startled when I unexpectedly saw one of the angels where I usually stand to prepare dinner. Surprised, I inhaled loudly. All right, I admit it— I gasped! I didn't mean to, but I was caught off guard. Try as I may, there was no taking back my reaction. Not wanting to upset me, the angel vanished and never returned. I was very disappointed as I never saw any of my angels again. I really do miss having them around.

Since my first session with Dr. Pearl and the angels that work with him, I no longer require any of the every-other-day blood transfusions which had characterized my existence. I also haven't used a wheelchair. Not once. I was able to walk and drive on my own. I drove myself to my third and final session with Dr. Pearl and have continued to improve ever since.

Even after the last angel left, I continued to reach new levels in energy, health and the overall quality of my life. I am once again doing all the shopping, cleaning and cooking for my family on a daily basis, not to mention chauffeuring my nine-year-old son around town and being den mother to his Boy Scout troop.

This is a big change for a woman who, a little while back, spent most of her time confined to bed. My sessions with Dr. Pearl have given me a new openness and allowed me to

25

absorb many new lessons. My feelings and emotions now run more deeply, more true. I have been left with a heightened sense of love, not only for my husband and my son but for the world as well. Perhaps the angels departure was their way of telling me that I was ready to fully recover on my own, that I was ready to care for myself and my family the way I always had.

I see myself as a survivor. A survivor is more than a person who merely lives through a disease. They are a person who has the courage to go on with life. It is enjoying family and friends, sharing love, being open to all possibilities, hoping, and always being true to your heart.

I am now 37 years old. It's been a long journey. I gave up my cancer in a millisecond, yet I will always cherish the lessons I've learned about myself—and live—as a result of my experience. It will always be my privilege to feel both happy and sad whenever I smell a vanilla ice cream cone.

– Contributed by Isobel Smith

PROTECTION FROM ANGELS

The scriptures are full of the dramatic evidence of protection from angels. Paul to the Ephesians writes: "Our struggle is not against the physical powers alone, but against the forces of wickedness in the heavenly spheres." The power of darkness and light have always been locked in intense conflict since the fall of the angels. Centuries later, we still have the opposing forces of goodness/light and evil/darkness.

An example of the protective role of angels is found in Acts12 vs.5-11. Peter is locked in prison awaiting his execution. James, his brother has just been executed and he has every reason to believe that he will be next. The magistrates of the day had ruled that Peter would be put to death in deference to those who opposed him.

As he lay sleeping, an angel appeared who was not deterred by the prison bars or chains that restricted Peter. Shaken awake, he was told to follow the angel's footsteps. Doors opened with the angel's intervention, and Peter ran out into the light absolutely free. If he had not heeded the force that pulled him in that direction he would have been executed. If he had stopped to question the validity of the experience he probably would have been discovered by the guards and executed anyway.

One could argue that Peter was in the wrong place at the wrong time, but it turned out that he was in exactly the right place and the right time. He believed he would not be spared, but others summoned the angels to help him to the

27

light, at a time he did not expect it.

Anytime you are surrounded by the forces of evil, you can generally know them by their divisive nature, rather than their unifying nature. The evil of fear, doubt, envy, greed, jealousy, lust and constantly being trapped in the rear view mirror of life without direction or purpose, are all signs of Satan in your earthly life. The nature of God is to move forward in complete trust in his will and divine purpose for your life just to learn about yourself.

In Daniel 6:22 we read, "My God hath sent his angel and had shut the lion's mouths." In the lion's den, Daniel perceived the angelic presence, and the lion's strength was more than matched by the power of the angel that came to Daniel's rescue. The angel had been sent to guard over Daniel and to overpower the forces of evil in the guise of a lion that fought him.

In these circumstances ordinary people thought that they were doomed or near to death. Why should it be different in your life today than it was in biblical times? Whether or not you believe in miracles is irrelevant. The forces of goodness always call the angels to intercede. I often wonder why we are brought into the darkness in order to experience the awe and majesty of the light? Maybe it is to teach us that there is more to understand. The story 'The Miracle and the Angel' shows the protection of angels in times of trauma.

Whatever you don't get by simple means, life will put you into traumatic means to get the message.

Dr. J. De Martini~

28

The Miracle and the Angel

By Dr. John F. De Martini

Do I believe in miracles? Yes! Do I believe these lighted, spiritual beings act as higher guides and messengers? Yes! Have I had personal experiences with angels? Yes! Can they help us experience healing miracles? They certainly appear to! Below is a story about Mrs. Esperanza who was diagnosed with lung cancer yet, after experiencing the presence of an angel, was miraculously and spontaneously healed.

I met Mrs. Esperanza in Houston, Texas in 1984, at a seminar I was presenting, entitled "The Healer From Within". At the end of this seminar, which was presented to the Cancer Prevention and Control Association, Mrs. Esperanza, approached me at the podium with a smile on her face and her heart and arms wide open ready to hug. She stated that she was so inspired by my presentation and that it was so beautiful to hear such a young man speak on such lofty topics as the power of spiritual prayer in healing. She said that she was healed through prayer and the message of an angel, and that she was looking for a doctor who understood such experiences. She requested one of my cards and gave me another wonderful hug as she was leaving.

The next day, Mrs. Esperanza appeared in

29

my Houston clinic. I was delighted to see her.
She had a special presence about her that was
most heartfelt and gracious. While taking her
history, she asked if she could tell me about her
miraculous healing from cancer. Although I was
going to become backlogged with patients, I felt
intuitively that I was to hear her story. She
demanded my attention, not out of insistence,
but out of her lovely and respectful presence.

She stated that almost five years earlier
when she was 64 years of age, she experienced a
gradual onset of a bloody, productive cough,
difficult breathing, fatigue and chest pain. At
first she assumed it was a cold, then she thought
pneumonia, but after her symptoms were not
showing any indications of improvement, she
visited her medical doctor. After extensive
testing and a battery of diagnostic procedures,
she was shocked to find out she was diagnosed
with progressive lung cancer.

She said it was one of the most frightening
moments of her life. She immediately felt
overwhelmed, confused, humiliated and full of
despair. She said she reviewed her life in a flash
and felt that somehow her cancer was due to her
life's many unloving actions. She felt her years of
sorrow, her times of frustration, her bouts of
anger and her blameful accusations. She said
that somehow deep inside, although she didn't
want to believe she truly had cancer, she felt a
connection between her unwillingness to love
and her present cancerous condition. Her years
of frustration about her financial circumstances,
her divorce, and her meanness to her own

children, were surfacing within her consciousness.

She said she felt that her cancer was somehow a compensation for her years of withholding her heart from people. She said this was such a low time that she felt she was dying when she thought about her condition. Suicide and isolation were running through her mind. She wanted to hide and never see anyone, just disappear with no one knowing what had happened. Then she said that she laid down and realized that her concerns were due to guilt and fear. She felt that if she was possibly going to die maybe she could somehow clear her consciousness beforehand.

She said her doctor recommended surgery and complete removal of her right lung since that lung was so infiltrated with cancerous tissue. He told her that surgery could have complications and that there was a possibility that she, because of her age and health status, might not make it through the surgery alive. This 'of course' added to her despair and made her even more determined to make peace with her children, grandchildren and loved ones. The night before she was scheduled to have her surgery, as a result of her request, she was visited by many of her closest loved ones.

As entered her hospital room, she embraced them one by one with open hugs and loving smiles. She shared with them what the truth was that had come her heart. She told them that she deeply loved them all, and that she was thankful for their contributions to her life.

31

Although her congestion, weakness and roughness of voice was difficult to understand, she said her heart was able to share its message clearly. She made peace with everyone who came and she asked those who were present to share her love and appreciation with those who absent.

After her loved ones left, she said she laid in bed and began to pray, more at peace and more grateful than she could remember ever being. About one o'clock in the morning she said she was awakened by an angel, and angel of light. She said this angel was like a beautiful young lady. She said the angel told her "that everything was going to be alright, that she was going to be fine, that she was healed." When she heard the message from the angel, she said that she began to weep, not out of sorrow, but out of exaltation. She said her face and body were immediately eased. She felt as if she was given another chance to live. The angel was present for only a moment, but the feelings were so strong that she knew that they would last. The rest of the night she laid in bed inspired. She reviewed her life and envisioned a new future. She imagined herself sharing her experience with others. She felt she was called by this angel of God to help others heal. She couldn't wait for morning.

At seven o'clock two nurses entered her room along with a man who was to escort her to surgery. When she told them that she would not be needing the surgery because she was going to be well. She said that she would like to check out of the hospital. The nurses were confused and alarmed by Mrs. Esperanza's statements and immediately called her doctor. After some time and confrontation, the doctor entered and tried to explain to Mrs. Esperanza that she must have the surgery to help extend her life. She told him that an angel visited her just hours before and that she was told by the angel that she was going to be fine now that she was healed. He became very concerned when she insisted that she wanted to go home.

The doctor was confused and angry and tried to talk her out of such foolishness. But she insisted and told the doctor that she would be glad to come back at another date and have herself re-evaluated, because she felt certain that she was going to be returned to good health. After a few hours of detail work, and the signature of hospital liability papers, she was released from the hospital and allowed to go home once her youngest daughter came to pick her up.

In the following weeks she said her lung congestion cleared up, her chest pains disappeared and her energy returned. In fact she was abounding with energy, like she hadn't felt for many years. She knew she had a purpose now to live for and began telling everyone she knew about her experience.

She gathered friends and family and told them that she was going to begin a healing ministry. Although, some of them wondered if that was the wisest thing to do, she knew that was to be her mission. At 64 years of age, she began her work of ministering to the sick and to everyone who would listen. She developed a following of listeners and people who she had helped. She opened a Center For Spiritual Healing. She incorporated whatever she learned and felt would help others heal. She taught from the chosen passages of the Bible and incorporated herbs and foods found to cause healing. She attended many classes on healing and this is how she met me, by attending my presentation at the Cancer Prevention and Control Association.

Mrs. Esperanza was truly an inspired woman, a woman with a mission. A woman who had been touched by the guiding message of an angel. Do I believe in angels? You bet I do! Do I believe these lighted, spiritual beings can act as higher guides and messengers? Absolutely! Have I had personal experiences with angels? I sure have! Can they help us experience healing miracles? They certainly can! What happened that night in Mrs. Esperanza's hospital room could truly be called miraculous. I believe it was a divine revelation and a visit by an angel. So expect a miracle and be ready for your message from an angel. A prayerful of love and gratitude is simply the way. May God bless you with such a guiding messenger of light.

Hebrews 11 includes long lists of people who have received miracles. They were delivered from disease, calamity, accidents and even death. Angels helped these great men and women to stop swords, defeat entire armies, quench fires and accept deliverance in their lives as a new way of life.

Do you wonder at the power of our healers who envision healing in our bodies before we can feel it, physically or mentally? Isn't this the summoning of angels as well? Isn't the intervention of wellness on a cellular level also an intervention of goodness opposing evil? Is it not possible that the healer can summon healing before we believe it exists? And not only envision it in us, but cause it to happen, just like the angels did, by their belief not our own.

It is a documented fact that abused women receive an average of 300 beatings before they leave a bad marriage, if they are not seriously injured first. Do they ignore the fact that their spouse is asking them to leave?

It is also documented that executives endure heart attacks, surgery and critical illness before they switch careers, change environments or end hurtful relationships. Do they ignore the pain and fatigue their body gives them until it is too late?

It is documented that children remain in volatile, emotionally unstable homes because they receive food and shelter. Accepting the abuse is the only life and the only love they know. It is also a fact that they repeat these behaviors when they enter into adulthood and their own marriages. Do they believe that abuse is the only expression of loving each other? Pain and suffering are considered to be normal in the human experience. Misery is completely optional.

Nothing has a stronger influence psychologically on the environment of children, as the unlived life of the parent.

C. G. Jung~

35

HOW HAVE YOU BEEN PROTECTED?

1. What event or circumstance occurred in your life when you were in the wrong place, in the wrong time?
2. Did you believe that you were unjustly or unfairly treated in the circumstance?
3. Did this obstacle in your life shake you so that you responded in a different way or make a different decision than you would have?
4. What divisive forces have been tearing you down rather than building you up?
5. What aspects of your past have you neglected to face and to heal? Do they keep showing up as signposts for your future growth?
6. What condition or circumstance are you enduring that repeatedly has asked you to leave?

What you argue for, you get to keep.
What we condemn is placed in our lives to teach us what we need to learn.

7. Has the inner meaning of the event changed your life?
8. Was light or goodness brought to your life?

The road to immortality is paved with the bricks of illusion. Tragedy is merely illusion. When we use these illusions to open up our hearts we receive miracles.

Part Three

Angels in Time and Space

SYNCHRONICITY IN TIME AND SPACE

*I*n recent years I've come to accept the synchronicity of events that occurred whether they worked in a positive outcome or a negative one. There was always a reason for a closed door as well as an open window.

In most circles synchronicity is defined as being in the right place at the right time with the right events magically falling into place. Experience tells us this is not always true.

Sometimes synchronicity is being in the wrong place at the wrong time and everything you have planned has fallen apart. Synchronicity experienced with magical events falling into place is as much an indicator of being in the right time and place as when the opposite events occur.

Events and their sequences point the way in

our lives in areas we need growth, development or sensitivity in our lives. That does not mean we need to analyze situations down to a microscopic level of responsibility. On the opposite side of the scale we must accept serendipity. It means we develop awareness to what works and what doesn't in the context of those events. The clue is to look for subtle changes in the energy surrounding the situation.

When the events or sequences of events do not turn out the way you expect, look at the situations that give you clues towards the future. While there is a delay, expect continued delay. Where there is no response or a negative response, leave the situation immediately.

Continuing the same behaviour invites pain into your life.

When there are a series of "no's", the universe is telling you to try something else that will be better for you. For example my friend, Samantha Wilde had a life long dream to move to California. She organised her life to prepare for the journey with two job offers in hand. She got to California and the college that was supposed to hire her to teach had not cut the budget for her position—nor did they bother to tell her that she did not have a position. Full of promise and expectation, she arrived in San Francisco eager to begin work. Not only did they not hire her for the job, she didn't get an interview with the president.

Did she get upset? No, she just got on the next train, through Santa Barbara to Irvine where she had met some friends. On the way, the train happened to stop in Los Angeles, Union Station.

Samantha is a small town girl from the prairies. Downtown Los Angeles was not a place she wanted to be. It terrified her! What do you do when the train conductor says, "This train does not stop in Irvine, Dana Point, or San Juan"? Clutching the little baggage she brought for the journey, she threw all her belongings off the train and sat down in the middle of the station crying. It had finally come to be too much.

A tall thin man approached her, "Can I help you, Miss?" he asked. She thought that he was another conductor. Seeing how upset she was, he gathered her luggage and negotiated with a conductor to put her on the right train in order to reach her destination. As he helped her to board he also said, "From this point forward, Miss, your luck will change."

She immediately met three different people who helped her make the decisions that changed her journey. The first was a senior advisor for the Disney corporation. His card led her to the people who hired her. Disney wanted her training abilities for their employees.

The second was a young woman who told her how beautiful it was in Dana Point. The third was an elderly gentleman whose sister lived in San Juan, perhaps she would take her in for a few days until she got settled. Samantha never did take any of the jobs she was offered, but started her own business and now lives in Newport Beach, California.

39

Was the tall thin man really a conductor, or was he an earth angel in disguise? If she had really been offered the job in San Francisco, would she ever have begun her own business in Newport Beach?

It's best not to try to interfere with, control or manipulate situations. The universe is clearly saying, "Do something different, look at a new side to this situation." There is another answer, just look for it.

Usually the answers are found in subtle events. A stranger often gives you clues that point to the answers you are seeking. A situation that was once positive for you or worked for you in the past may reappear and work for you again, when you give up your need to control the event, situation or person. You finally give up, usually in despair.

Many times I had a feeling of connection to my environment or happiness although there seemed little explanation for it. I moved to a century-old home in the country in order to begin my writing career. I remember the second day. I said, "Brigitte, I have a feeling that you have in your library the research materials I need to write my book "Quantum Energy".

She said, "Why don't you look on the shelf over there?"

I wasn't surprised at all when I found stacks of material on time and space, interconnectedness and physics. Brigitte had been given these books by her father. They had been written many years before by mystics and seers in India. By coincidence the books were

Chance is always powerful. Let your hook, always be cast in the pool where you least expect it. There, found will be a fish.

Ovid~

40

exactly the research I needed.

To make coincidences even greater, when I moved back to the city I visited another pair of friends, Lilli and Erwin. I said, "I know you have books in your house that I need to write the opening chapters for, "Are You Ready For A Miracle With Angels." Within minutes I had ten books on angels, several versions of the Bible, copies of the Dead Sea Scrolls and Judaic and Roman theology. Would you say that I had been placed in these environments on purpose? Did I choose these places knowing in advance that the materials I needed would be there? Likely not! Did I choose these places innately on a spiritual level because the energy was right, and if the energy was right, the other things I needed would be there, too.

When I threw out my own agenda, listened with an undivided heart and heard the promptings of the voice of God given to me through angels, miracles happened. They happened quickly and in a way that was more complete and perfect than I could possibly have planned in my own imperfection. It was an easier way to reveal the answers I needed for my life.

SYNCHRONICITY

Think of examples of synchronicity in your own life that have made the way easier. Here are a few others from my experiences.

1. A woman discovering she wants to reshape her body goes to a gym to exercise. On her way there she meets an old friend at aerobics class who works out regularly and invites her to exercise with her. Not only did she lose weight, she had fun with her friend.

2. An entrepreneur had a terrible first quarter in business. Everyone was calling for money. Just as he walked out the door on Friday night with his last twenty dollars in his pocket, he receives a phone call that a check for a thousand dollars is on it's way for a deal he had forgotten about. It's the first of several checks that began to arrive without effort on his part. He turned his business completely around with that one situation.

3. A minister wanted to go to Montreal for an interview at a new church. He does not have enough money for the trip. A friend currently visiting gives him two coupons for train tickets that she happened to have in her purse. The minister and his wife travel to Montreal where he is successful and receives the appointment at the church.

4. A real estate agent is cold-calling for listings one evening. She telephones a woman who complains vehemently about her last agent.

Other people do not create your spirit. They reveal it.

Brandt~

Her house has been for sale for almost a year. The agent solves the problem for her, does not get involved and says good-bye, never expecting to hear from her again. Two months later the woman calls the agent who lists the house and sells it in three days. It changed the life of the woman and the attitude of the agent. The agent realized how much those cold calls helped people.

5. A student desperately wanted to be a pilot. While on vacation in Colorado, his mother visits the Air Force Academy and asks a few questions about enrollment. A year later, her son accepts a scholarship and goes there to study, fulfilling his dream.

6. An author, just finishing a book on miracles, is telling an old friend about the book. He smiles and says he has just been invited to host a television show on Miracles, Magic and Mystery. Would she be available to talk about the miracles in the fall on television?

The show has millions of viewers. The book changed the lives of the viewers. The show changed the life of the author.

Talking to Brigitte about synchronicity, she told me how she had found a book about her father-in-law whom she had never met. She was in a flea market one Saturday looking at books. On the top shelf was a book that kept "blinking" at her to reach up and look at it. Just as she began to leave the shop she thought, "I must look at that book quickly before I go."

The shopkeeper took the book down and

Seek and you will find it. What is unsought is also undetected.

Sophocles~

43

said the price was ten dollars. Looking inside, Brigitte noticed there were several references to pilots in the war. Her father-in-law had been a pilot in the war and had died two months before Brigitte was born. She had never met him.

The book looked interesting so she bought it and sat in the car to wait for her children. She opened the book and there was a photo of her father-in-law, Albert von Schwerin, as he stood by a plane in World War II. He had been decorated with the Ritter Cross for heroism.

Tears of gratitude flooded her face. You can imagine the shock of her husband, Joachim, to see pictures of his father who had died when he was ten years old. Can you believe that she found this book by listening to her intuition? No one in the family knew the book existed or that her father-in-law was in it.

Brigitte paid attention to the messages and returned to buy the book. She listened to the message of her inner voice for guidance. She was rewarded in a way she did not expect for following her inner voice . . . her guardian. When was the last time you listened to yours?

If you don't believe that the world can give you the glass slipper like Cinderella received, you need to have the faith that a glass slipper is available in your size and Prince Charming is waiting to dance with you at the ball.

Ask for the miracle, an angel will supply it. Synchronicity daily reveals the will of God in our lives.

ANGELS OF INSPIRATION

When angels appeared in Biblical times they were so glorious as to stun and amaze those who witnessed their presence. It is completely fascinating that angels appeared regularly long ago, but in modern times their appearances are rare. Perhaps we rush about too much. They could show up much more often in all their magnificent glory if we exercise patience. I think it must be because we don't expect angel visitations. We don't have friends come to visit when we're too busy to take the time to chat.

Perhaps, when we begin to recognize the earth angels around us as real in our local culture we would receive insights into experiences that are not fulfilling. We would see a direction for change. Angels may also be bringing us messages which are more advanced than we can understand today. If we listened and obeyed the message, our perception of humanity would also change. Our earthly accomplishments would be enhanced and the frequency of miracles on earth would increase a thousand fold.

Plato said:

"The newly initiated who has a sight of the celestial vision, when he beholds a God-like face or physical form, first of all shivers and experiences something of dread, which the vision itself inspired; next he gazes upon it as if it were a God, and if he were not afraid of being thought an utter madman, he would sacrifice to the beloved as to the image of divinity."

Our purpose is waiting for us to "wake up" to it.

Angelica Wagner~

45

I have often wondered why we get shivers at thought of greatness. We get shivers when someone says something that is particularly insightful or true. I have wondered if it wasn't an angel showing up to give us an insight into something that we needed to learn in that moment.

Angels manifest change in our lives by giving us thoughts that cause us to rethink our direction and to lead us by inspiration. I was at a seminar where Tony Robbins was speaking about ecstasy in our lives. I listened as a very small man in a wheelchair sitting behind me said it would be ecstasy for him to walk again.

Although it had been many years since I had regained the ability to walk, I remembered in a flash the pain of those six weeks of confinement to a wheelchair. The small man became my earth angel in that second. Tony Robbins became my earth angel later as he insisted that I write a book about the experience. I learned that I love to write books about real people and real miracles.

I had not attended the seminar with the purpose of a complete life change, but I received one none the less. From that day forward it became my mission to write stories of miracles. As I travelled collecting these stories the transformation in the people that I spoke with transformed me. My experience in a wheelchair opened my heart to understanding of a love for humanity. My experience with tragedy opened the door for a career I did not seek. It found me. What have you found that you were not looking

To those who by persistence in doing good seek glory, honour and immortality. He will give eternal life.

Romans 2:7~

for that was good for you? Did a messenger of God send it?

FROM INVISIBLE THOUGHT TO VISIBLE CREATION

When you throw a pebble into a pond, the ripples expand through to the other side, eventually creating waves on the opposite shore. When you sing, dance or laugh, the joy that you project into the universe eventually comes back to those around you. This energy is reflected by your posture, your voice and in the very fabric of your cells. You become your soul energy. This soul energy is projected to everyone you speak with, live with, spend time with.

St. Augustine said, "It is the name of the indweller, not the temple." Does this mean that we can access the angels within, if we understand the knowledge of our soul?"

If thought precedes matter, as the great philosophers have established, then does it not also follow that the invisible precedes the visible? Thought can be projected into matter. Just as the pebbles create ripples in the water so do thoughts create things in our world. Have you ever thought about someone and then that person calls you or shows up in a place you did not expect to see them? Have you ever dreamed a wonderful dream or had a vision of accomplishment and then saw these visions unfold before your eyes? That's how our Olympic athletes accomplish feats beyond themselves. That's how all great people accomplish great dreams by first visualizing the end result.

To accept the responsibility of being a child of God, is to accept every good thing that life offers you.

Stella Mann~

Inspired moments are grateful moments.

Unknown~

47

If this is the case do we need to pay particular attention to thoughts, actions, desires and the emotions within as we experience them? Because sooner or later, they will show up as real in whatever form our imagination has envisioned. Imagine good long enough, and only good follows. These feelings and emotions imprint on our cells as we feel them. If we could give our thoughts to the angels and keep them in charge, it would be interesting to see what wonderful things would manifest as a result; thoughts focused on spiritual things rather than earthly things. It would be interesting to see the results if each of us could be in tune with our heavenly natures within by accessing our own angels. This creates daily miracles in our lives.

Whenever I have been in tune with, or empowered by my own intuitive connectedness or innate powers, the calamity passed through my life more quickly than if I tried to fight against it. Intuitive connectedness happens when your inside voice tells you how to handle the problem even if it's in a way that's different.

It was understanding this really bad thing had showed up to teach me something I had neglected to heal before. When I paid attention to whatever it was, and gave it the acknowledgment that it needed, but did not allow any negative energy, the calamity passed through quickly without hurting me physically or leaving an imprint in my cells. When I tried to deny what was going on in my life and passed it off as unimportant, it always came back again

Your inspiring dream takes you past the obstacles.

Dr. J. De Martini~

to visit me more in greater doses of trouble. When I paid attention to people who were bad for me and acknowledged them, but did not associate with them, they left my life quietly. My life, over time, was transformed by better people and coming situations, when I learned to say "No" to the situations causing me pain.

Angels manifest change in our lives by planting in our minds the inspiration for self transformation. Those choosing to hear the call of knowledge will be transformed by their own angelic experience and bring light and goodness back to the world in their communities and families.

The next story is about someone who experienced brain tumors and lymph tumors. Rocky wrote this story himself and submitted it for this book. Thinking about wellness, he now leads a normal life.

I hope this story opens your minds and hearts to understanding the importance of honoring the body and the soul's need to love. Probably, if his need to be well for the family had not been strong, the results would be different. He believed he would be healed and was grateful to be on the *Road Home* to his family.

All electromagnetic frequencies alter matter.

Albert Einstein~

The Road Home

Contributed by Angelo "Rocky" Russo

In September 1991, my wife and I were blessed with a baby boy. The following month, I was in the hospital getting a total thyroidectomy. I had thyroid cancer.

I was in excellent physical condition prior to surgery so my recovery time was minimal and I immediately went back to work as a self-employed contractor. As the days and weeks passed, the thought of having cancer would occasionally surface. Being a new father, however, I quickly forgot any of these concerns. I healed completely and continued to work as if nothing had ever happened.

In January 1992, as we were coming home from a wedding, my wife and I found ourselves in an evening snowstorm. As we sat at a red light, we were suddenly struck from behind by a drunk driver. We both sustained neck and back injuries which required that we have MRI tests taken (sort of an advanced form of x-ray). One evening my doctor called and informed us that my MRI had revealed more than just herniated discs. I had a tumor in my head located in my pituitary gland. My wife and I were devastated. We didn't know what it all meant.

I was sent to a specialist in New York City who examined me and explained that 99% of the time these tumors are benign. He further stated that since this type of tumor often tends

Your desire is your prayer. Picture the fulfillment of your desire and you will feel the joy of answered prayer.

Dr. Joseph Murray~

to shrink on its own, he would not operate right away. The plan was to get an MRI of my head done every six months, just to keep an eye on it. We were relieved and satisfied with his opinion. Every six months I went for my MRI and life went on.

In the late winter of 1994, I began to experience head pain different from anything I had ever known before. This was no ordinary headache. I went to a neurologist for an examination and was told I was experiencing "cluster headaches". Due to their severity, cluster headaches are commonly known to drive people to suicide. They would come and go in flashes. I also had a steady pain up the back of my head that literally pulled the life force right out of me. The pain got so bad that I was bedridden.

Eventually the pain became so severe that I returned to the neurologist. This time the neurologist himself brought me to the hospital for an emergency MRI fearing that the tumor had hemorrhaged. Fortunately, the tumor had not hemorrhaged. It had, however, grown significantly and surgery was required immediately.

In May 1994, I was scheduled for brain surgery. You can't imagine the anxiety that comes with the anticipation of having someone operate on your head. My surgery lasted three hours and the tumor was successfully removed. Recovery was long and tiresome. Unfortunately, when you tamper with the pituitary gland it stops functioning. Since this is the master gland which controls most of your body chemistry, I was now

I used to pray that God would do this or that; now I pray God will make His will known to me.

Chiang Kai Shek~

51

chemically dependent. Every day I had to take four doses of hormones and 30 mg. of hydrocortisone. In addition, I had to get a testosterone shot every three weeks. My doctors told me that if my pituitary gland did not regain function within a month after surgery, I could expect that it never would. It didn't. Again, my wife and I adjusted to the new routine and life went on.

One day I was watching a television program about healers. I was not familiar with an alternative form of healing so the idea interested me greatly. Since the medical world had already given up on me, I decided to pursue a healer in an effort to get my pituitary gland working again. I've never been one to go down without a fight. Even though the gland had been non-functional for several months, I was determined to find a healer and make myself whole. The search carried on for over a year.

In June 1995, I was at my periodic cancer examination when my surgeon fund a tumor in my right neck. A cat scan and MRI confirmed that the thyroid cancer had spread to my lymph nodes. Surgery was scheduled for July. I kept myself and my wife on a positive track by thinking that I would come through this operation successfully and all would be well again. My search for a healer had to be put on hold temporarily.

Surgery lasted for five hours. It was a radical dissection of my right neck. Eighty-eight lymph nodes were removed and of them 22 were cancerous. The surgery was very painful and took almost three months to heal. Once I recovered from this operation, my search for a healer began again. I was determined that after three major operations in less than four years, I was going to get back to normal.

My search finally climaxed when NBC in California responded to a letter I had sent them regarding a show I had seen on healers. Several names and addresses were mailed to me. I reached those that I could, but the one who really made an impression was Dr. Eric Scott Pearl in Los Angeles. I was excited! My search was over. I was finally going to have a session with a bona fide healer!

In November 1995 my wife and I met Dr. Pearl. My pituitary gland hadn't functioned for over a year and a half. Medically speaking all hope was lost. After explaining my condition, I had a private session. It was a genuine experience. He held his hands over my head. After several minutes, I felt a tremendous heat and finally passed out. Upon awakening, I was quite disoriented. He explained that some results tend to be immediate while others may only become apparent with time. He asked that I write or phone to let him know of my progress as it was the only way he could keep track of things.

In December 1995, about three weeks after my session with Dr. Pearl, I started to experience new and unusual feelings in my body. My doctor confirmed my instincts that I no longer needed my medications. Under supervision, I began to wean my body off the drugs.

After three months, I am now 95% drug free with a well-functioning pituitary. My doctor and I are hopeful that I will soon be 100% drug free. Test results are now normal. I'm feeling great. My stamina is better than it has ever been, even better now than it was before my surgery. My spirits are high. My wife and I are once again leading a healthy, normal life.

After receiving my most recent set of normal laboratory results, I smiled and asked my physician what he now thought about healers. Following a moment's contemplation, he replied, "The only thing I can tell you is that there are a lot of strange phenomena out there that I really don't understand."

After sufficient time had passed and confirming medical tests had been completed, I contacted Dr. Pearl to inform him of my results. He was truly happy to hear of my healing.

As a father and self-employed contractor, it's a luxury if I find time to make it through the morning newspaper, let alone ponder the mysteries of the universe. Yet on the rare occasion that I do have a free moment, I often try to make sense of all the wonderful things that have happened. I've come to realize that there are a lot of strange phenomena out there that I don't understand. One thing both my medical doctor and I do understand, however, is that I was healed that day. I don't like to brag about it, I don't need to justify it, and I guess I don't even have to understand it. All I know is I've got my health back—and it's been a long road home.

Earth has no sorrow that Heaven cannot heal.

Sir Thomas Moore~

Part Four

Gateways to the Light

TO LIVE WITH MORE LOVE

*P*lato in the Symposium wrote, "This is the right way of approaching, or being initiated, into the mysteries of love, to begin with the examples of beauty in this world, using them as steps to ascend continually, then from physical beauty, to moral beauty, from moral beauty to the knowledge of supreme knowledge and absolute beauty." All truly great historians and leaders did their earthly work with love. It enhanced their work. It gave them joy and energy. It transformed the energy of ideas into knowledge and finally knowledge into reality.

"The angels will lead the elected to their blessed end, where they will be lifted up and carried, as Elias was on an angelic chariot amidst rays of heavenly light". This verse from Enoch I:2-4 carries the message that those who live

I cannot believe that the inscrutable universe turns on an axis of suffering; surely the strange beauty of the world must somewhere rest on pure joy!

Louise Bogan~

with love will be lifted up to a higher level. The message, whether earthly or divine is always to live with love. **Only the work of love will lead you to immortality.** It is the power of love that gives you the energy to accomplish all things. It is the power of love that is the highest, finest and fullest expression of who you are. Love is found in the activities we give our attention to and is what we make time for every day.

If you are living with people you love and who love you, you'll be able to give that love back to others. You'll be able to find greater peace and acceptance in everything you do. If those you are living with are not in harmony with you, not in love with you and your earthly purpose, your heart and spirit, you will always feel that you are not enough. The interesting point is that if they don't love all of you, the good, the bad, or the indifferent, you will never be able to please anyone no matter what you do or say.

Living in an environment of love and acceptance is not only critical to your happiness, it's critical to your health. When your heart is unhappy, sooner or later, disease creeps in as the only way to fight back.

Disease knows the only way to make up for the lack of love in your life is to find you the attention that you crave in a hospital bed.

If you are in love with your work and enjoy it, you will find time to do the details or carve out the vision, if that is what's necessary. You'll do anything to accomplish your dream, no matter what it is. If you love your work enough,

Love is not blind. It sees more, not less. Because it sees more, it chooses to see less.

Rabbi Julius Gordon~

nothing will stop you from success.

Financial abundance will follow because you have given it heart energy.

If there is constant interference in accomplishing your dream, it's necessary to have a chat with yourself about the people and surroundings where you have placed yourself. Sometimes it hurts to say "no" to people you thought you loved. Sometimes it hurts to drop friendships where issues cannot be resolved. Until the necessary changes are made you stay where you are. All resistance slows you down and you stay stuck.

When you surround yourself with those who contribute to your heart energy you can really move forward with all systems on go. Resistance slows you down. Anything you are not in harmony with, from your heart out, will stop you from being your very best. Create harmony in every interaction or pay the price of playing catch up while you watch others with less talent, ability or creativity zoom forward. This works in all areas of human endeavour. It works in all areas of health. It works in all ares of a relationship.

The following is a story of a mother's love for her child—it showed her making some unpopular choices because the health of her child was more important than what other people thought. The health of her child and her family caused her to make the changes she needed to create a miracle in her life.

Our Miracle Son

Contributed by Marie-Claire Groulx

Children are born every minute of every day. They are created and given to parents sight unseen. It is up to us to choose how we raise these little people, regardless of the difficulties life may throw at us.

On the day we moved into our new home, my family physician confirmed that I was pregnant. We were very happy. The pregnancy progressed and the nausea subsided, but in my tummy, along with my baby, was another growth, something growing bigger and faster than the baby. At around four months, I was referred to an obstetrician. There were a few days to wait for an appointment and I experienced intense abdominal pain during one of these nights. People had been praying for me. When I saw the doctor the following day the growth had disappeared mysteriously.

Time went on and I soon became huge. At seven months I began contractions; three minutes apart then one minute apart. I went to the hospital frightened that I might lose the baby. I was put on an alcohol drip then injected with lung-stimulating hormones for my baby. After five days of bed rest I went home.

At eight months I was readmitted with a dangerously low estral level—below the life-death level. We pulled through this stage and went home after six days of total bed rest.

Finally, three days after my due date, I began labor. My water broke and strong contractions began near midnight. We went to the hospital and contractions continued, one minute apart, from 12 a.m. till noon, then 30 seconds apart until they decided to "section" me. I was in shock, my baby was in a breach position in fetal distress. I was at four centimeters, tired and scared. After an epidural I was wheeled into O.R. and given a quick section while I was awake. Our beautiful, curly haired, pink son was born perfect and healthy. In my womb they found a large scar; a remnant of whatever had been growing there: A MYSTERY, A MIRACLE. Francois came home after six days. He had been quite jaundiced but nursed well.

Time went on and he gained quickly, but he was a real fussy baby and any change would upset him.

He began getting his teeth at three months and was very ill with every tooth. At six months he was admitted to the hospital with a diaper full of "bloody mush." He was so ill. Every doctor in town, it seemed, had seen him and couldn't understand. The next day he cut three teeth at once and felt better. The fever went down and he began to drink again.

He was up and down, often sick. Our family doctor was concerned with his slow growth pattern, low weight, his many colds, his persistent earaches, infections, etc. We were frequent visitors at the doctor's office, but no other options were offered to us. We did the best we knew how. Francois' hearing was sometimes less than 40% in his early years in school. He was treated by an ear, nose, throat specialist for several years. He had tubes in his ears and a tonsillectomy after several pneumonias. At age six, after several bouts of infection, he had a circumcision. Post-op infection meant a long stay in hospital.

At age seven, he spent nearly five months total in hospital for several bouts of asthma, pneumonia, lung collapses, etc. From this point on, he was considered a chronic asthmatic.

We went to Ottawa for a visit to a special clinic for lung disorders. He was treated with a variety of medications.

From age seven to fifteen, Francois was a frequent visitor to pediatrics at St. Joseph's. On the average he had four or five pneumonias a year and three or four collapsed lungs aside from everything else: chicken pox, flu, infections, etc. He was taking seven to twelve different kinds of medications a day; one, two, three, four, six times a day. Physiotherapy was part of our home routine. Life was one day at a time for those eight years. Our whole family life revolved around health and trying to achieve it.

Our pediatrician was a wonderful support to us. Nonetheless I was always open to new ways of improving my family's health. During the spring of 1994, while visiting a naturopathic doctor for myself, I received hints about caring for asthmatics, changes in diet. Francois visited the naturopath and was prescribed a bottle of a homeopathic preparation to stimulate the metabolism in his digestive system.

After having seen many doctors in North Bay and Ottawa for a recurring neurological disorder and still having a poor quality of life. I decided to try a chiropractor in addition to the naturopath. I chose Dr. Thomas Preston. Within a few visits I noticed a remarkable improvement in my energy level as well as my coordination. I thought immediately of Francois who had been diagnosed with scoliosis and asked Dr. Preston if he would consider treating him. Treatment began within days.

After six months there was no more medication, no colds, no more asthma. Wow! Life force surged to stimulate his immune system. One year nearly to the day after a double lung collapse, a subcutaneous pneumothorax in his first days of high school, Francois and I learned he had officially no more asthma. He had been given a ten per cent chance at best of outgrowing this kind of asthma in his life. But quality of life is improved. He is now medication free. Even his dentist has seen an improvement in his oral health. Medications do have side-effects that linger in the system. No more.

In early December of this year, Francois woke up feeling very poorly. With early cold symptoms, I was concerned that he might become very ill as he had many, many times before. Off we went to our chiropractor's office for an adjustment. He seemed to stabilize but rapidly deteriorated within twelve hours. He woke up on a Saturday morning with a partial lung collapse. I telephoned Dr. Preston at home

Love is a great thing, goes above all others, which maketh a burden light.

Thomas Kempin~

61

and within the hour he was being adjusted. We went home thankful. We exercised. We walked while deep breathing. We drank a lot of water. After six hours, Francois was breathing normally. His lung had reinflated. He was tiring easily, but able to rest comfortably. What a miracle. When the life force switch is turned on, health is enhanced. We were created to be well, not to be ill.

We are still aiming for physical growth. To have suffered as he has and be where he is now is truly a miracle. We love him dearly and continue to be amazed by his progress.

THE ANGEL OF LOVE

Transcendence into the next dimension is found in the Gateway of Love. There is nothing more glorious on earth than travelling to the light. Spirit leads us to the light when we need to make changes.

It is the Angel of Love that visits us when we are in most turmoil. This angel loves each of us enough to whisper into our ears when we are not loving ourselves as much as we should, either by the company that we keep or the work that we do, or any other interference in our happiness.

We are loved by our Angel of Love. When we listen, she opens doors of opportunities at the time when we are ready to accept them. It is written that the grace of God cannot lead you to a place where the will of God cannot keep you. Where does the will of God in your life need you to be? What has happened in your life to convince you that you are not loving yourself enough?

It shows itself in revealing goodness, light and happiness to you. I think the Angel of Love is the instrument of making God's will known to us. Whatever you love, you will take time to be with. You will be blessed by the Angel of Love loving you.

1. Have you ever lived in a place where no matter what you tried to accomplish it never reached your expectations?

Whatever a man loves, that is his God. For he carries it inside his heart!

Martin Luther~

A gem is never polished without friction. Nor is a person perfected without many trials.

Unknown~

2. Has your body ever been in a state of pain, where even one more day of pain would be too much?

3. Have you ever watched someone you loved be sucked into a vortex of drugs or a surgery from which you knew there was no return?

4. By remaining in a situation that gives you pain or leaving you exhausted emotionally or physically are you loving yourself?

5. Are you actually half-comatose or half alive in your daily existence? What drugs or alcohol use contribute to your half-death? If you are not feeling totally alive . . . why? Are you breathing?

6. If the Angel of Love could write a love letter to you, what would she ask you to change? Pretend you are the Angel of Love and write a love letter to yourself.

If any of these questions have been answered with the realization that you are not loving yourself, maybe you should start now. Perhaps you will learn to love others more deeply and with greater compassion. Where there is pain in your life you need greater compassion. Make a change until you feel loved and appreciated. Set boundaries and limits with everyone to get what you need.

Tell the truth in a loving and kind way, yet firmly respecting yourself.

When you start to raise your awareness, the most appropriate good will show up for you. You will notice an association with those things you love and a death or non-association with those

It is a beautiful necessity of nature to love something.

Douglas Ferrola~

What I am saying is that we need to be willing to let our intuition guide us. Then be willing to follow that guidance directly and fearlessly.

Shakti Gawain~

things or people that are not in your purpose.

It's actually very simple.

Follow your intuition about the direction you yearn to follow then leave the rest in the past. Physically remove yourself, if you must, from the situation until you get the message. Then move forward deliberately, fearlessly.

GATEWAYS OF THE UNKNOWN

In mythic terms, Eros, God of Physical love and Thanatos, God of Death, are twins. We imagine Eros appearing as a lovely youth and Thanatos appearing as a frail dying form. In the Greek myths quite the opposite is true. Eros shows up as a figure of death and Thanatos shows up as an adolescent. It intrigues me to understand that both love and death are gateways to the unknown. This reveals their eternal adolescence, and the eternal youth of their emotions.

When you are in love, you believe that you can do or accomplish anything. The rites of passage into love are absolutely parallel to the rites of passage into the next world. In death as in love, we are out of our present selves and someone larger than ourselves takes over. A new identity is formed. Like oxygen and hydrogen together they form a totally new substance, water. We are not always sure where the journey of love will lead us, or whether or not we will stay there, but we always travel through a rite of passage as the intermediary stage to the gateway. There we become transformed.

There is a feeling in your heart. If you don't do what you were sent to do . . . you will die without it.

Dr. J. De Martini~

He who knows others is wise. He who knows himself is enlightened.

Tolstoy~

65

The gateway brings transformation. In many instances we are completely transformed in our realization of being in love with someone, another human whose soul we have merged with in a more seductive merging than simply one of the flesh. It is as though the spirits have joined and become one self. In many ways it is a death of the self. In the search for truth, the reality that the self you once had and no longer exists can be terrifying. Yet the new being completely transformed, separate yet joined, shares the essence of divinity in the union. This transformation creates eternal joy—heaven on earth, a state of bliss.

The moments of ecstasy in physical love involve complete surrender in the pleasure of love, giving death to the ego of the self, swept up in the bliss of the body and soul union with another. The ecstasy of being in love is also a surrender to the being of that relationship above all others. It places the relationship with the beloved in a sacred place above all relationships, save the relationship with God. The sweat of the physical passion being the only sweat needed to resolve the tensions in the relationship.

The essence of marriage, therefore, is to live together in love and harmony, in truth and light. This union of love forms a partnership that is entirely new together, joined but having separate identities. The union of love being God's intention for men and women from time of the garden of Eden. This separateness actually being the glue that binds the partnership, the space between the soulmates creating the excitement

The meeting of two personalities is like the contact of two chemical substances; if there is any reaction, both are transformed.

C. G. Jung~

Love is more than a characteristic of God.

Deuteronomy 7:9~

and constancy in the relationship, like the polarity of two magnets drawn together; opposite yet apart.

Bliss is a state of complete harmony and union with your soulmate. God created Adam and Eve so that we could know about soulmates. He took bone of Adam's bone and flesh of his flesh to create Eve, another dimension to Adam. This eventually created the war of the sexes. The state of being in love is a state of disorder in our lives of surrender to the emotions. Love complicates life. It makes us selfish.It causes us to be interested, vibrant, happy and contributing to our life purpose.

Love creates transformation.

All love stories are about the meaning of our own existence. The ability to transcend ourselves and merge with the infinite, or rather the divine, in our lives, there is magic. Transcendence causes expansion and growth into new dimensions. In transcendence, transformation finds divinity.

Part Five

Exploring the Dark Side

Wealth lies not in the extent of possession, but in the fewness of wants.

Hebrews 13:5~

Those we hold most dear never leave us. They live on in the kindness they showed, the comfort they shared, and the love they brought into my life.

Norton~

ANGEL OF DEATH

The angel of death, in turn, is as seductive as the merging of two bodies in the earthly realm. It is mentioned in rabbinical lore that the Angel of Death has such a seductive gaze that the soul is withdrawn from the body at the time of departure, as if by a lover to the next world. The body is literally seduced to travel into the next dimension by the eyes of this angel. The seduction of the soul being rapturous into the next world.

Have you ever watched a person that you loved die in front of you? The pain is not in the experience of death for the person dying, it is in the sorrow of those who are left behind.

Often as humans we view death as punishment for a life that was not fully lived, rather than a transition into another dimension. This dimension is one that we have earned, one

68

that enhances us rather than diminishes us. I believe that the Angel of Death is one of the kindest and gentlest angels. This angel has been especially chosen to accompany humanity on its journey to meet God. This angel transcends the space from earth to heaven and cradles the humans in his arms as he carries them to heaven.

To allow the body to transcend, to give the body permission to rest is to give death the honor and respect it so rightly deserves, rather than to continue in our own human ego and will. Death is a state that the body must embrace. When our earthly work is finished no matter what that time frame is we need to accept death with respect and gratitude.

The inner spirit always knows when it is time to move on. We need to learn to listen and rejoice in this call to greatness, rather than to mourn, weep and wail for a form that is past.

Just as we lose control of the body in the ecstasy of physical union with our soulmate in the gateway to love, we also lose control of the functions of the body in the gateway to death. Slowly, before the transition, the body begins to shut down its functions. The heart stops beating, the lungs give no breath, the intestines expel toxic waste and so on. The body prepares to give itself up, and the spirit prepares to move on to a better place.

Thus the message of love, like the message of death is always one of order. To know love and death is to know everything all at once. In this body and out of it, **the heart opens you up to the really big stuff in your life.**

Shared joy is joy doubled. Shared sorrow is sorrow halved.

Unknown~

Maximum involvement occurs at the crossroads of chaos and order.

Dr. J. De Martini~

69

- Accept the transition. No matter what your fears are. It's supposed to feel scary and uncomfortable.
- Movement from the known to the unknown is a sign of a gateway to transformation. Move with it, even though you may not see a destination. Believe it will be good.
- Transformation removes pain from our lives and takes us to a state of bliss.
- Chaos is normal in a state of change; accept it. Accept the vulnerability. Learn to integrate your fears into the new experience. Be humble to the intelligence that runs the universe. Listen.
- The inner spirit always knows when the transformation will take place. Learn to go into silence to find the answers.
- Get out of human ego and accept the blessings of both love and death. Greatness and goodness emerge. Accept the new state as uncomfortable at first, even traumatic. It takes time for the body/mind to adjust.
- Nothing mortal can stop anything immortal.

My soul finds rest in God alone; my salvation comes from him.

Psalm 62:1 ~

Since we were created in the image and likeness of God is it not fitting that those who belong to God should be returned to Him at the completion of the journey?

Have you allowed someone you loved to move forward with death in love and honor?

Is there a death in a situation or circumstance that you are holding on to that is keeping you from achieving greatness? Is there a death in a relationship you are holding on to?

Is the inner spirit calling you to move forward to something better? Are you doing the things you need to bring order into your life?

Are you holding on to chaos? Why?

THE FALL OF THE ANGELS

The most brilliant and beautiful of all the heavenly angels was Lucifer. He was the ruling prince of the universe under God. As written in Ezekiel 28:12-1; "You had the seal of perfection, full of wisdom and perfect beauty, you were the anointed cherub and I placed you there. You were blameless the day you were created, until unrighteousness was found in you. You corrupted your wisdom by reason of your splendor." Thus Satan represents the fall of both wisdom and divinity in the soul.

In the second book of Enoch, the account of the fallen angels is synonymous with the fall of the stars, this points to pride as the reason for the fall of the angels. Satan wished to set his throne higher than God's and so he was cast down along with his followers. Satan refused to obey the word of God and for this was banished from the Divine Presence. The myth of Satan and the fall of the angels is the myth of man's separate identity from God, the separation being the Ego. Although the ego or human will is not a bad thing, it does keep us separated from our Creator. In being separate from God, we are without wholeness in our own Divinity.

Lucifer had creation at his feet and yet this

was not enough for him. His purpose was the glorification of God but instead of serving Him, he was not satisfied. He lusted for power, for that which belonged to God alone. I look at Lucifer in the same way that I view anyone on earth with a lust for power and control as being completely destructive. It is the insatiable lust for power in all relationships that causes disease on a cellular level. It causes cellular and molecular implosion in the body in the same way the atom bomb causes implosion on earth. The lust for power in relationships also imprints in the very fibre of our cells and stays there until we discharge it.

- Why do we choose to defy nature in seeking means of restoration of our earthly form that is antagonistic to the body on a cellular level?
- Why do we choose the internal warfare of drugs or chemicals to establish order into a sphere meant to ring with the breath of life?
- Why do we choose drugs to numb the symptoms rather than dealing with the causes of the problems? Why do we believe that drugs were meant to heal us rather than to harm us? Do the drugs know the difference between the healthy cells and the diseased cells? Or do they kill all cells?
- Why do we invite surgical intervention as a means of cut and paste to deal with problems that can be resolved internally by honouring the body, mind and soul?

- Why do we consciously or subconsciously seek relationships that are destructive rather than constructive?
- Why do we not seek relationships that rebuild us and are nurturing rather than a struggle for power and control?
- Why do we reinforce human ego and the will of outside hostile forces, instead of admitting that we are wrong or have chosen incorrectly?
- Do you realize that you can always choose again in harmony with who you really are? You have the power of choice.

FALLEN ANGELS IN OUR CELLS

1. What belief do you currently hold to be false?
2. Who is the Lucifer in your life that is holding you back?
   What situation is holding you back from greater good?
3. What has this evil done to you on a cellular level?
4. Have you ever felt a tingling in your hands, feet or body, sneezed, coughed, experienced cramps or diarrhea, or headaches recently? This is your body discharging forces of evil. Listen to your body's voice.

Do you cover up the symptoms with aspirin, pain relievers, cold medicine or other pharmacological interventions that are chemically created to dull the senses not enhance them?

73

Do you repeatedly get sick because of a situation, relationship, career, or place of residence that you have chosen for yourself, yet your body tells you it is not congruent with either your health or your spirit?

Pain and suffering are normal in our world today, a life of misery is optional.

FALLEN STARS OF HEAVEN

The power that created the body is the power that heals the body. It remains our life force energy that was God-given and then lost in the free will that came back to man in the temptation in the garden.

The war in heaven sprang from a group of angels who freely chose to sin and a group heralded by Michael the archangel who chose to worship their creator. God cast the sinful out of heaven but they still survived. It is said that two thirds of the angels remained in heaven to continue the work that God asked of them. The rest of the angels were banished, as Satanic messengers.

Where have these fallen stars gone? Where have these fallen angels of darkness disappeared to on the earthly plane? If angels never die, are Satanic angels present in our life today?

If Satanic angels have the power of concealment, does that mean they show up in disguise as good things in our lives when they intend evil? Question the presence of disease in your life. Question the presence of chaos in your life.

Successful discharge involves our body/mind's system going from higher tension to lower tension from a state of distress to a state of ease.

Donald Epstein, D.C.~

74

1. Have you called the friends of righteousness or the friends of evil to help you to your full potential? Do you have supportive allies in your life or do you surround yourself with poisonous playmates who try to hurt you by offering destructive advice or saying mean things to you? Do you have friends that deliberately sabotage your success? Do you help them by telling them all your plans?
2. Have you allowed destruction on a cellular level to reap havoc in your life? Have you invited disease into your life by choosing to surround yourself with people who hurt you? Have you invited disease into your life by staying in a relationship, career, location that makes you unhappy?
3. Have you looked for signs of order in your life to verify that you are in the right place at the right time and with the right people?

FORCES OF EVIL IN OUR LIVES

Like other angels, Satan can assume many forms. In a blink he appeared in the garden to Eve as a snake. By causing doubt in her mind about the clear intentions of God he caused her to eat the forbidden fruit. Revenge being his sole purpose, Satan caused the fall of man, changing history forever. The angels of darkness cause disorder in everything they do. That's how they make themselves known to you. St. Paul to the Ephesians states, "The Prince of power of the air worketh in the children of disobedience." Unrighteousness and transgression against God is

75

self-will against the will of God. Does it not follow that to stay in a state of disorder and chaos either mentally or physically imposed, is to stay in a state that is in ego and not in the intention of God?

Since one third of the angels transgressed the will of God to follow Satan they constitute a mighty force of evil in our midst. Not only do we live in a perpetual battlefield of disorder, but the invisible war of Satan's rage wastes human resources, corrupts moral standards and is poised to contribute to the fall of the nations. The nature of the angels was that they received ever-lasting life. Imagine the drama that the fallen angels play in the war of life on earth with the creation of their everlasting evil! Imagine the war of life with the continuation of destructive forces rather than unifying forces in our universe! Imagine the fact that these destructive forces of evil are alive and well in our current world and disguise themselves in order to fool us!

Are you paying attention to the factors that move you forward in your life or are you content with the destructive forces of evil holding you back from your true potential, physically, mentally and financially?

We stay in situations that are uncomfortable long after we should. We stay there not because it is uncomfortable, but because it hasn't killed us yet. It couldn't be so bad. Wrong! All evil imprints on our cells and in our hearts and causes us pain. The fact that it causes disease is not yet an accepted fact.

If the body regenerates itself almost completely every three months, don't we also have the power to regenerate goodness, rather than perpetuating evil? If on a cellular level we can regenerate and transform, why can't we use the disguise of poverty, illness, or relationship war as signposts that we need a better future, rather than remaining stuck in the disease? Do we not also have the power to regenerate our lives to abundance and fullness, rather than to destruction, chaos and evil if we choose to associate differently?

- Have you asked yourself about the importance of negativism in your life and why you hold on to it?
- If you are currently a few pounds overweight are you holding onto negativism to keep the pounds you don't need?
- Have you asked yourself if the people, situations and environments that you have chosen are helping you or in the will of your own ego's and hindering you?
- Is there chaos or disorder in your life? Why?
- Do you intend to wait until the end of your journey, death or terminal illness to see the folly of your ways or can you do something about this situation here and now?
- If you are witness to the forces of evil in your life are you questioning these points?

Learn to get in touch with yourself and know that everything has a purpose.

Elizabeth Kubler-Ross~

1. What lesson is this situation or person trying to teach me?
2. Are the forces surrounding this situation ultimately unifying or ultimately destructive? Unifying forces create miracles.
3. Will surrender to the situation cause it to change? Will confrontation of the situation cause it to change? Do I need to change?
4. Will the removal of my ego cause a correction or a shift in the situation? Am I causing the situation by what I am doing, or what I am not doing? Silence is an answer.

Try to think about how the answers to these questions will not only change your life but also the lives you currently touch. Take these lessons not only in your family, but your community, your country, your world. Let global peace begin with internal peace for each of us. Global peace begins with peace in the family.

THE WAR WITHIN

Sin is a fact of life in our world today. It is manifested by selfishness and sorrow, broken hearts, broken dreams and lost souls. It shows itself in disease created by a war within. Satan's strategy is to rationalize that war is a normal state. Are conflict, turmoil, disorder, toxic waste, illness in the environment in speech, thought and deed simply a part of life as we know it or are they the transgressions of Satanic influence in the world?

The war within the body, the transgression

The masses promote fear and guilt. Evolution is the intelligence of the universe run in your heart. That's where evolution begins.

Angelica Wagner~

78

of Satan on a cellular level is a separation from wholeness, a separation from God, a separation from love in the universe. It is a separation perpetuated today in order to cause not only disease but disharmony, disunity and disorder in our lives.

I grew up with conflict as a normal state in the condition of my life. Living in the home of an alcoholic father and an invalid mother constant conflict (due to the expectations that were never met) on both sides was the order of the day. Finally, rather than confronting the situation and creating my own life at eighteen, I ran off with a man I thought would bring love and peace into my life. Within six months, I realized I had married someone whose spiritual state was totally nonexistent. The forces of complete disrespect reaped havoc in my life and the life of my children as a result of my impetuous decisions. It was years before I woke up to the fact that this was not going to change —until I changed.

I could not imagine how I would ever earn enough money to leave this relationship and yet to support my children at the same time. They were all very young and needed a full-time mother, not someone who worked hours and hours selling real estate. I struggled for years both emotionally and financially with the impact of this decision. Once the decision was made, I moved on. I learned to be successful because the only other option was poverty.

At the point where I uncovered evidence of a potentially abusive situation with my second

Trust in yourself. Your own perceptions are more accurate than you believe.

Unknown~

79

child, I just couldn't ignore the situation, or hope that it would go away any longer. It's amazing that the longer that you live in a destructive environment the more you get used to it and perceive it as normal. It was as though I had become totally numb to feel anything, because if I dared to acknowledge the pain, it would have been so overwhelming that I would almost die from it. I couldn't remember a moment of joy in my life for years. I couldn't remember the emotion of happiness. I couldn't ever remember feeling carefree. Today I can't believe I ever lived that life.

Within six months of being on my own, I found myself in a wheelchair unable to support my children at all. I had self-fulfilled the prophecy, my worst fear. I had let Satan win the internal war. I hadn't listened to my inner instincts in order to find the way to truth and ended up in a car accident that showed me the stuff I was really made of. I now know that this situation was brought into my life in order to make me the person that I am today.

I found the courage to walk again. It took being told that it was highly unlikely that I would walk again. After three adjustments on my spine I moved my foot. Within six weeks, I was walking again. Years later, I still jog and maintain a more active lifestyle than most people. Years later I discovered that in order to reach optimum health, I had to say no to those elements in my life that were causing me harm, regardless of what anyone's opinions were. I also had to say no to situations and people that

If I am worth enough to be reprimanded, I am worthy enought to be praised.

Unknown~

The best way to get even is to forget.

Matthew 5:44~

80

caused me harm, regardless of who they were.

When I learned to travel only with those who were congruent with my purpose the journey became less rocky. It is almost as though those travelling companions felt my energy and decided to accompany me and those who would cause me difficulty, controversy or emotional distress soon disappeared from my life, never to be seen again. I began to wonder whether I had not become too boring a companion to my former friends or were they ever friends?

We will continue to live with pain in our lives until we realize that there is an easier way. Until we choose to listen to the message of love in the   universe, pain, suffering and the war within will continue. The forces of evil have only one commitment: to destroy, to divide and to conquer.

Beware of those who come into your life to give you grief rather than to help you to your higher purpose. If you are on a path that is not helping or healing take a look to see who is travelling with you. If it's not God or an angel, you may never arrive at your destination.

It's important to observe our lives from the outside in, rather than the inside out, because when you do, the powers of goodness will come forth to help you, and the destructive forces eventually get the message and run for the hills.

Guard well your heart... for it is the well spring of life.

Proverbs 4:23~

Happiness, I have discovered, is nearly always due to a rebound from hard work.

David Grayson~

HALTING THE WAR WITHIN

1. What is causing your heart to be broken today?
2. Is your body sending you a message to make you change?
    a) your environment
    b) your food habits
    c) your relationships
    d) your work
    e) your lifestyle
3. What are you separated from that could bring you joy?
    a) your soulmate
    b) a new home
    c) a new career
    d) a new belief system
    e) forgiveness
    f) gratitude
    g) abundance
4. Why have you chosen to stay with that which is causing you pain? Is it that you can't leave or that you won't leave?
5. What difficulty, controversy or emotional distress keeps coming up to head you off track from what you really wanted to do?
6. Have you made a list of five activities that once gave you joy?
    a) playing as a child or with your children at the amusement park
    b) dancing
    c) staying out all night or sleeping in all day
    d) a walk on the beach
    e) scuba or sky diving

Thus does the world forget Thee, it's Creator and falls in love with what Thou has created instead.

St. Augustine~

f) sex

g) just having fun

7. What is the worst thing that could happen if you changed one thing that caused you pain?

8. What is the best thing that could happen if you changed one thing that caused you pain?

9. Are there travelling companions on your life's journey who are healing to you or are they harmful?

10. What are you denying in your heart and soul that causes you to remain in a stuck pattern?

11. ***To whom or what can you say, "No," so that life says, "Yes," to you?***

The creation of something new is not accomplished by intellect, but by the "play" instinct acting from inner necessity. The creative mind plays with what it loves.

C. G. Jung~

$\mathscr{P}art\ \mathscr{S}ix$

$\mathscr{L}adders\ of\ \mathscr{A}scension\ to\ \mathscr{M}iracles$

No emotion is expressed without the opposite emotion being repressed.

Dr. J. De Martini~

The burdens that appear easiest to carry are those borne by others.

Galations 6:2~

LADDERS OF ASCENSION

*F*or people who continue to live in pain either from an injury, chemically self-induced illness, or living an unfulfilled life is a result of cellular imprinting on a body that is at war. When the inner spirit is at war the body is at war. In order to cope to survive the body begins a war within. It is caused by lack of love in our lives and that lack of love permeates our being until either accident or illness take their toll. You cannot escape the war at a cellular level if you are not living in harmony. If there is turmoil, anger, fear, or despair in your life, you are at war within.

If you consult with a whole life healer, you will be told that disease is imprinted into our bodies through stuck patterns which we accept on an emotional level as normal yet on a cellular level our bodies don't accept this message. These stuck patterns show themselves in our spines, in our cells, in our emotional states. They show themselves by inhibiting our freedom of expression. No flexibility in the body, is expressed by no flexibility in our relationships, our work, or our soul.

I thought I had beaten the destruction in my soul on a cellular level when I walked again. Little did I know that pain and suffering imprints on such a deep soul level that less than a year after my accident and the death of my mother, I had the opportunity of contracting real disease. I was not growing on the outside in both my life and my career so my body/mind took over to teach me a lesson. I lived in an environment that diminished, controlled and abused my spirit. Yet I refused to acknowledge that something was wrong with my life. I thought that by pretending and acting as though my life was a field of daisies, magically this would be true. Guess what? It wasn't. I had to face the truth. This relationship was destructive rather than nurturing to my spirit. If I chose not to make the changes that my body demanded, it would kill me. What situations are you facing that are hurting you on such a deep heart level that you have become physically ill because of them?

Rather than face the truth, I became ill. That pattern on a cellular level had imprinted into my body and it created an internal war. My body began to reproduce internally what I was fighting externally. Would you think it co-incidental that I showed the same symptoms of the same disease, (ovarian cancer) that took my mother's life? It was completely congruent that I had already experienced this. My cells patterned themselves into warfare. I will never admit to having had a disease. I even refused to discuss my condition with my children until ten years later. I escaped by finally making the changes in my life that my body demanded to keep me healthy and whole. I changed my life because I listened to my body and heard my inner voice, my guardian angel. It was time to make some major changes in my life, to move forward with confidence, rather than with fear that somehow it would all turn out alright. Once I had decided, it did. Ten years later I am in impeccable health and have more energy than ever.

The secret of life is that it is God-given.

Psalm 2:7~

MY TRANSITION TO THE LIGHT

I had minor surgery that ended up as a major event in my life. During the operation, I almost died. The rite of passage that I experienced, travelling toward the light was the most glorious experience that I have ever had. The light was so bright and beautiful. It had a luminescent quality that was beyond my imagination. I felt completely peaceful and serene. I felt completely joyful. The light was so radiant that I was completely seduced by it. The relief of being in a place of complete weightlessness and ease called me away to the journey. I could not believe how magnificent the light was and I wanted more than anything to follow it.

As I looked back on my body, still on the

operating table and heard the conversation in that operating theatre, life called me back. One of the nurses said, "It's so tragic, what will become of her four children?" In that split second, the love for my children completely outweighed the power of the light and that beautiful serene place that beckoned me. I knew that my work on earth was still incomplete. The rite of that passage transformed my life on earth completely. In those few seconds, at the gateway of transformation, I knew that from that moment on I had the power to be the author of my own manuscript.

In merging with death and accepting its rite of passage in my life I actually found life. I found a self that I had been denying in the sheer energy of raising an active family by myself. When I finally gave up the need to control my life and accepted the passage into another dimension, my true self emerged. In giving up mortality we accept the gift of immortality. The human form of my being was transformed by my immortal spirit one that needed the trauma to change.

It actually took years for me to accept this passage as real rather than just dismiss it as "imagination." It took the trauma of near death to really accept living my life to the fullest. The lessons I learned are just emerging now as my new life begins.

I realized that if I could die at any given moment I had better do the things I wanted to do immediately and love the people that I loved without bounds, restrictions or conditions. It

There is a time for everything, and a season for every activity under heaven.

Ecclesiastics 3:1 ~

87

took death to make me understand how precious life is.

- The state of being alive is a brief transition, a temporary period in time and space. Live it well.
- We experience triumph only by going through and accepting the tragedy not by going around it or dismissing it as unimportant.
- In order to receive the light you have to accept the darkness as real.
- The death of the old self creates room for a new divinity within. It is your birthright to claim it.
- In order to achieve greatness you have to give back to the universe the life and hope it has given you.
- In transformation it is realized that when all matter is raised to the spiritual level you find your real truth.

I am including the next story, far more dramatic than mine could ever be to emphasize the point that the body does have the intelligence to heal itself. When Jean Brown Wetterlin did as I did, removed the garbage and baggage from her life she stopped living in fear. She took the first step to creating a miracle in her life. I hope you do, too.

The Big "C"
And it doesn't stand for Cancer

By Jean Brown Wetterlin, D. C.

My name is Jean Brown Wetterlin, D. C.
The D. C. stands for "Doctor of Chiropractic"
and it's because of the basic beliefs that
chiropractic is founded on that I am alive today.
I was diagnosed, during surgery for what my
medical doctor thought would be routine
removal of benign muscle tumors of the uterus,
with polysystic adeno carcinoma, stage 3-C.
What this means is that I had a very advanced
case of ovarian cancer. This happened on
October 23, 1992.

During this surgery, removal of my ovaries
omentum (the outer fat layer that protects your
pelvis between your hips), uterus, tubes and
residual tumor that they could get to took place.
I was told that my right ovary was the size of a
volleyball and that my left ovary was about
grapefruit size and had grown into the pelvic
wall. The only symptom I had observed was an
odd feeling (no pain) in the lower left quadrant
of my pelvis. This was probably due to the left
ovary beginning to pull away from the wall of
the pelvis as that tumor grew and gained weight.
My surgeon did take out as much tumor as she
could, however, there was still tumor left in me.
The places mentioned in the surgical report
were as follows: on top of the bowel, in the base
of the pelvis, implants of 3 to 5 centimeters

89

under my diaphragm and on top of the dome of the liver. The fluids of the pelvis tested positive for microscopic tumor cells as well.

After surgery, I was sent to an ob-gynon-cologist at the University of Minnesota who reviewed my case, pathology reports and did a physical examination. I was then told that I had one year to live, 6 months without pain. He recommended that I get started with chemo-therapy right away, and that I could gain additional months. I told him that I was a Chiropractor who believed in the body's ability to heal itself and was considering alternative recommendations. The oncologist blatantly told me that if I did not follow his advice, I would be back within 6 months in severe pain, begging him for what he had to offer. Needless to say, over the next 2 weeks I struggled with what decision I should make. What I decided was based on the fact that I would not let fear dictate my choice but rather would make my decision on what I know to be true.

Chiropractic espouses that the body has within it an intelligence to care for itself. It is a natural occurrence, and is able to function, without help, as long as there is no interference. I looked at my life and started to unload the garbage and baggage I was carrying, mentally, emotionally and physically. I decided to go to Juarez, Mexico to a facility called the International Medical Center where I was evaluated and examined and started on a regiment of care for one month. This routine included procedures that are considered noninvasive and enhancing to the body: ozone therapy, laetrile (vitamin B17, which is illegal in this country), nutritional considerations and organic sources, shark cartilage both orally and rectally, coffee enemas, reik machine, aloe vera, thalamine and fetal animal cell shots to stimulate the immune system to kick in. Chiropractic adjustments, colonic therapy, massive dosages of vitamins, and massage and hydrotherapy for relaxation. Each person at the Center was treated individually.

While there, I also saw another Doctor outside the Center who was using a product that a nuclear physicist invented. The physicist had been employed by the U.S. government and was retired. He developed intestinal cancer with the same cell-type that I had (adenocarcinoma). Everything that I did had the basic premise of helping my body to help itself and worked with enhancing my body's own abilities to heal. As of last December, all blood tests showed no cancer growth, and even the most intricate imaging done by MRI and CT scans show no cancer. These past three and one half years have been relatively pain free, I've been able to continue my work as a Chiropractor and live my life to the fullest. I am tracked by a pelvic oncologist in St. Paul who shakes his head at me and says that in twenty years of practice, he has never seen another case such as mine. I am writing a book that will probably be named **IT'S THE BIG "C" . . . AND IT DOESN'T STAND FOR CANCER,** which hopefully will be finished before my five year survival date!

91

ASCENSION THROUGH HEALING

How often do you hear about massacre, violence, racism, killings, bombings, addictions? Day after day doesn't all this bad news imprint in our hearts and souls a message we recreate? Miracles are also a normal state of being. I began to wonder why bad things were coming up not going away. Was I ignoring what wasn't working? Covering it up with workaholism?

Covering up all the bad with the lies of perfectionism that didn't exist in reality? What was really going on under the surface and why?

I believe that we call pain into our life in order to learn about joy. Without pain, we have no staff of comparison for the blessings that are meant to be the basis of our divine birthright. For every tragedy there is an equal or greater triumph. Besides calling the angels, blessings and miracles into our lives, we need to believe that we deserve them. It is our right to experience both joy and abundance for the simple reason that we exist . . . nothing more. How do we get there? Look into the pain for the answers.

All we need to do is examine our heads, bodies and our hearts to monitor what is going on there. Out with the pain, in with the joy!!

In order to reveal our deepest love, we must be willing to reveal our deepest pain.

Angelica Wagner~

THE NEED FOR CHANGE

Are you asking yourself:

1. What destructive forces have I accepted as normal?
2. What have I numbed myself into believing contributes to my life?
   How am I dulling the pain instead of feeling the pain so I learn to change?
3. Have I brought illness or disease into my life by denying my inner life spirit?
4. Am I perpetuating a stuck pattern because it's easier to accept than to do something to change?
5 . Am I seeking love as the answer to heal the pain? Is this love that I am seeking a cause of the pain I am experiencing?
6. How can I love myself better in this situation?

If any of the answers to these questions cause you to think twice about your life, it means you are still able to create change. **Problems come to challenge us to respond by expanding our horizons and cause growth.**

THE VOICE OF ANGER

Anger has a voice. It is meant to be listened to and respected. Not only does it show us and others where our boundaries are but it points the way to improvement in our lives. Sometimes when someone says something that angers you

You divide the confrontations into success in order to get paid.

Mark Victor Hansen~

93

or hurts you very deeply, the message usually means you are not paying attention to your inner needs. What angers you, shakes you up to understand that your inner needs are not being met. What angers you, really shows you where your deepest needs are. What angers you really shows you where you have encouraged neglect and abuse in your life.

Anger is not meant to be ignored. It is meant to be acted upon. It takes us to a new direction, sometimes one we had not seen before. When used as a guide the reasons for anger need respect. Action is the antidote for anger. Do the opposite of what causes you anger and it will be gone from your life.

If there is either a person or a situation that continually causes you anger, why do you go back to the same well for more of the same water? Either resolve the situation or remove yourself from the source of the anger. ***Patience is not a necessary ingredient here—Respect is.***

If you do not respect yourself enough to confront the situation in a loving manner to resolve it with someone you care for, resolve to banish the negative from your life. Dirty laundry requires some bleach.

Why do we feel that giving the unhappy situation more time will bring it to resolution? WRONG!! Giving the unhappy situation more time encourages it to continue, increase, grow! Like yeast in bread unchecked anger grows under the surface to erupt when least expected or wanted.

Go often to the house of a friend: weeds choke an unused path.

Ralph Waldo Emerson~

Other people don't create your spirit; they only reveal it.

Brandt~

To handle anger, look upon it as your very best friend.

What angers you, conquers you.

Deal with it or it will deal with you.

It will continue to provide you with the same lessons, in the same manner, until you learn to deal with it. Do something.

Anger is always a direct reflection of those qualities we like least about ourselves that we mirror onto other people.

Ask yourself:

1. Why am I angry?
2. What steps can I take to take care of myself in this situation?
3. Who or what do I need to forgive?
4. What or whom can I be grateful to for causing me to perceive things differently?
5. How can I bring love to this situation? Who do I need to confront to resolve this situation?
6. By getting on with my own life and my own goals how can this situation change?
7. Have I given this situation too much time or too little time?

Is it time to say "NEXT"?

The life which is not examined is not lived.

Plato~

Part Seven

Transformation Through Miracles

WHY DO MIRACLES OCCUR?

*T*o reinforce the divine nature of
humanity . . . we are in divine
likeness to God.

To balance tragedy with triumph, evil with
goodness, selfishness with unselfishness, yin and
yang energies.

Synchronicity in the encounters or the events
and the way in which they take place.

A feeling of complete darkness or despair in
the current situation a feeling that nothing can
solve or help the current dilemma.

A dream that is unexplained, an intuition, a
contradiction in the nature of the environment
or a vision that is in direct contradiction with
current occurrences.

Total surrender to the consequences of the absolute worst happening in the situation. Acceptance of tragedy illuminates acceptance of the miracle and gives the miracle the opportunity to appear.

An unexpected kindness or message from an unexpected source, at an unexpected moment. "Isn't it interesting you called?" Always related to a current concern or problem troubling you now.

A feeling of peacefulness and resolution to the problem or situation. The situation may not have resolved itself or worked itself through, but you feel that it will because of the signs you have seen.

HOW MIRACLES OCCUR

There is no order of difficulties in miracles. At any time, in any place miracles can occur when you invite them in. Asking for the miracles is the same as inviting a good friend in for tea.

All you have to do is ***ask for the miracle*** and allow it to happen on its own.

When we make the ***shift to natural healing, miracles*** will happen with greater frequency.

When you ***choose to be healed,*** you will seek healing from the inside out rather than the outside in. You will understand all trauma, emotional or otherwise imprints in the body to cause disease.

97

Acceptance has the *magical quality of empowerment.*

As we give we receive;
Ask yourself.
> If you are only for yourself—what are you?
> If you are not for others—who are you?
> If not now—when?

Purpose in life awakens you to service.

A shift or counterforce of energies. An inversion in the paradigm of thought. This shift will come from an unfamiliar source. Miracles will begin to show up as more people talk about them.

Society that is *wellness expectant* rather than disease expectant. Society that accepts miracles as opportunities for the illumination of our own divinity . . . *The God source that is within all of us.*

Miracles occur as the process of healing and correction in our bodies and our hearts as a result of the shift in thinking that all things are accomplished *with love.*

Every problem that we face in humanity today is caused by:

a separation from wholeness
a separation from love
a separation from purpose
a separation from human divinity
a separation from God within

Miracles are the **counterforce to create a radical shift** in the thoughts and actions of a humanity dying as a result of the lack of **life force energy** and love in our daily lives.

Heaven is the awareness of perfect unity within the universe here and now.

THE AUTHENTICITY OF MIRACLES

In the retail world of the 90's, the consumer often seeks actively for an authentic product. We search for brand name labels whether that may be in our perfumes, our shoes, our watches, even our jeans. We look for an authentic sign that this product is real. We believe it to be real because there is often a label on it showing us that the product was made by this designer or that manufacturer. When we buy jeans they normally come whole not with patches on the knees. When we buy new things from a store, we pay for the newness of the product. Sometimes, we even believe that new things are better than the old ones and that good products generally come whole and in one piece. God created miracles in our lives to prove that broken, battered, tattered and torn lives have as much right to a miracle as those whose lives seem perfect.

By means of miracles, God manifests authenticity to the world. Miracles are a sign or a sign action that God has chosen to intervene. These signs show the reality of God as His true self. By means of miracles, God bears witness that He has sent His messengers, the angels to

Everyone thinks of changing Humanity. No one thinks of changing himself.

Tolstoy~

attend and to prove the authenticity of that miracle. This element of divine intervention addresses to humans an urgent message of the will of God. Miracles prove that God is real in our lives. That the work of God is authentic. The angels are sent to attend to the miracle so that His vision for our lives may be unfolded. When we accept miracles as signs and more importantly as actions, the miracles become the label, that the product came from God and belongs to us as His children and His heirs.

God does not send us miracles to patch up our lives, like we put patches on our favorite jeans, to make them wearable a little bit longer. He gives us instead, a whole new garment, a whole new self. That means we receive a completely new attitude and often a completely new body to authenticate the miracle. God doesn't go just halfway into our lives. He's looking for His own product with His own brand name on it. His own label is authenticated and recognized by the power of love. This is the most complete sign that He has been present. This is the most complete sign of a miracle. Watch for signs of love around you.

Whether we believe that we deserve this miracle or not is entirely irrelevant. We receive because we already are perfect and enough because of who we really are. We are creations of the divine. No matter what anyone else thinks about you, or says to you, you are already great and very deserving of all good things. Begin to live your life that way.

Whatever miracle you need in your life;
ask for it and expect it.

We become completely new creations when
we are the recipients of miracles. The intention
of God in our lives is to reveal, authenticate,
reform and revolutionize life. Repairing you
with a little patch as you think you need it won't
revolutionize who you are. The miracle is sent to
transform you. The miracle is sent to create a
new being and a new life for each person that
the miracle touches. This includes the family and
the extended family involved in the miracle.

Throughout his work on earth, Jesus was
known as a healer. His healings was an action
that inspired by the love of those people who
needed him and believed. The reason we were
created was for deep and never ending love. It is
the same reason that we are created to have a
deep and never ending love for each other. The
greater and deeper that love that is displayed in
your actions, the deeper and greater the
possibility for life transformation. Have you
ever loved anyone deeply enough that they
produced a profound change in your life? Have
you ever loved your work or your life purpose
enough to devote yourself totally to it, to be so
lost in it that you lose track of time. This is also
life transformation.

God always knows exactly what we need
when we need it. If there is a need for a healing
in your life, he will heal you. If there is a need
for love in your life, he will show you a place
that you may give it, in order to receive it. One
of the miracles of universal law is the law of

101

giving—as you give so shall you receive. Your needs for a miracle will be addressed. Your job is to believe it and ask for it. Keep on asking until it shows up—often unexpectedly.

Miracles have happened as an intervention in the paths of destruction that we humans have chosen for ourselves. The next story is one of complete healing .

I have included in this book numerous stories of healings that have taken place. The shift to healing is a shift that will change the world in its outlook on health and the causes of disease. In the same way it took centuries for scientific facts to be accepted, flights to the moon and computers to be accepted, the truth on transformation will take time to be accepted. The truth on human healing outside of the allopathic model also will take time to be accepted.

The next story of love actions shows the true nature of the transformation. *In the authenticity of love actions, the label of God's presence is always found.*

Start to look for circumstances and people that show you love in real ways and you will eliminate disease, disaster and tragedy in your life. You will stop the 90 yard dash towards chaos and begin embracing harmony. You'll start to love your life!!

- In what area of your life do you need a miracle?
- In what area of your life can you create a miracle?

- What greater power was revealed to you?
- Are you peaceful about the result?

A feeling of complete peacefulness always accompanies a situation surrounded by love. ***This is energy creating the miracle.***

Dear Angie,

Thank you for taking on such an adventure as your new book. I wish you luck and many blessings. I have had a miracle happen to me as a result of chiropractic care that I would like to share with you.

I suffered from severe asthma as an infant. From the time I was born I had constant asthma attacks and was always in and out of the hospital and/or medical doctors' offices. I had to sleep on a slant with my head elevated. Someone had to watch me 24 hours around the clock because I would frequently stop breathing and they would then have to take me into the bathroom and turn on the hot water to let the steam open my blocked air passageways. I was constantly on medication and getting worse.

One day, when I was about 18 months old, I was released from the hospital and my mother was told that they had done all that they could do for me. They suspected some other type of wasting disease such as Hodgkin's disease and suggested some tests. They told her that it was just a matter of time now and that I probably had one or two months to live.

That very afternoon, a neighbor came by and suggested that she take me to Dr. Charles Jones, a chiropractor in Torrance. She had spoken to my mom before, but since my mother was a nurse, she would never take her son to one of those "quacks". This time, however, there was nothing to lose, so she took me to see him.

After examining and X-raying me, he determined that my atlas was jammed up against my skull. This seemed to make some sense to my mother since during labor, I was starting to come out while she was still in the parking lot. The nurse put my mom on a gurney on her side, pushed me back in and sat on my mom's legs until they got her up to the delivery room.

Dr. Jones adjusted my atlas, a bone in my neck and sent me home. Within a few hours, I began coughing and spitting up tremendous amounts of phlegm. My mother said she could not believe there was that much inside such a small baby. I improved rapidly and within a week I was perfectly normal. The doctors couldn't believe it, and when told it was due to chiropractic care, they refused to give it any credit.

I have continued to receive adjustments regularly the rest of my life and from that day on never knew that I ever had a problem. I was very active in sports in high school and had no limitations whatsoever. When I was 17 years old, my mother finally told me the story and *that's when I decided to become a chiropractor myself.*

– Contributed by Donald J. Baune, D.C.

105

ANGEL HEALERS

C. G. Jung wrote that every patient that falls mentally ill has lost sight of that which basic religions teach: a sense of emotional healing and a deep fulfilling sense of being loved. This is the work of our earth angels, often appearing as ordinary people in the disguise of healers.

Although I have had the privilege of working with and being in the presence of hundreds of healers, I have not met one who did not feel called to his mission. Their purpose is to love and to serve humanity. Their mandate is not just to heal the body but to endow it with the health of new vitality, energy and life-force spirit. Here we are most emotionally starved and physically starved.

The Bible states that is in the will of God to create humans in his own image; all powerful, all creative, all serving, all loving. It take conscious effort to go against the voices in the world in actualizing the healing powers of nature. It is much easier to believe that the cure for illness is external rather than intrinsic. That we should just take something, swallow something, administer something, cut something rather than unleash our own personal potential in the creation of wellness and wealth in our lives. The power that created the body has the power to heal the body. The aching soul is a reflection of the body in torment.

The negative ego dwells within us and the darkness of fear surrounds us. The more our internal world is illuminated, the more light will be brought to the world. This is easily done by embracing our finest nature. By reaching first for natural means of healing, we are saying to ourselves and to the universe, "I have the power to heal myself, and that is where I will begin."

It all begins with a declaration of sovereignty in the body and the soul to regain our independence through natural means, rather than surgical or pharmacological intervention. It is claiming our own autonomy that we reclaim the divinity of our souls. The true life force energy does not come in artificial implants, containers of drugs or even in plasticity of emotion.

It comes from the reality and challenges of being human.

At the most basic level angels are sent to heal the anguish of the human heart, to teach us that we are never alone. Through their presence we can know that we are not rejected, not isolated, not fearful, not in pain. Once this relationship with God through the angels grows and matures in your life, you will experience unlimited power and ease in everything you do . . . especially as your life purpose is unfolded to you.

Until we experience pain, we do not experience humility. The source of humility then becomes transformed into a source of strength. To go within is not to turn our backs on the world but to honor the internal essence of our true power, the interrelationship of body, mind, heart, spirit, and soul in order to reclaim our own personal sovereignty. Healers acting as earth angels bring us to true purpose by the liberation of our spirits through the liberation of our internal power.

Inner listening enables us to understand that our first love must be to ourselves. The connection to the heart center allows us to feel balance in our lives. As balance occurs, windows of opportunity open. We facilitate our own healing. The chemical changes of the detoxification process allow us to let go of what we earlier could not release. In discharging this negative energy, we may move into chaos for a while, but it is important to move with this chaos rather than try to control the symptoms.

Discharge is the call to change. It is a massive awakening of the body that change is necessary and imminent. The tension of unresolved feelings accumulate in the body/mind. These tensions are resolved through discharge.

Anything that no longer serves your highest good can be discharged from your body from your life. Any aspect of the self that no longer contributes to healing can be and should be let go. The body expresses fever in illness, pushes out blood or pus in infections, causes vomit or diarrhea in intestinal turmoil, fluids in orgasm. The body creates headaches, backaches, or illness to tell us that on a cellular level there is trauma—there is chaos. Chaos in our bodies is a good thing and should not be masked by drugs.

Chaos in our bodies reveals the need for change. The cut and paste of surgery does not remove the need for internal change. Until the

internal tensions are resolved, the body continues to manifest chaos.

Chaos is essential for meaningful healing and change to take place in our lives. The newfound energy in changing allows us to redirect our lives in harmony with perspectives we have gained. Energy is regenerated in resolution. When we learn to use this internal energy in change, our lives move forward at an unbelievable pace, very much like a rocket taking off.

The discharge process, like cleaning the closet, is significant. The internal awareness of realignment with the natural order causes the body to show signs of stress. Threat to the physical body is caused by the underlying truth of unresolved chaos in our lives. This transitional stage is enroute to the transformation. Rather than masking it with drugs we need to feel it.

That means enjoy the process, the pain, stress and chaos whatever your body is showing you as Truth.

How is your body showing chaos or a need for discharge?

How do we respond?

Do we apply a bandaid, an aspirin or drugs, surgery or alcohol; or do we embrace the illness, the accident, the failed business deal, the unsuccessful romantic relationship as an urgent call for change?

Then we have the courage to move forward in confidence with the changes that are needed to be made in our internal lives.

Like the gardener pruning the roses in the fall to prepare for the new growth and blossoms of the spring, change must be evident internally before healing takes place externally.

External victory is always preceded by the acceptance of internal Truth.

TRANSFORMATION THROUGH FINDING PURPOSE

I met Heather in line waiting for the theatre to begin in Santa Barbara. She was introduced to me by a bouncy young student of theology, with masses of curls, called Katharine Brown. I was intrigued that Heather had just come back from spending three months working in a hospital in India. She was invited to speak at church that Sunday. Even more intriguing was the fact that these strangers had also invited me to be there for the occasion. They were amazed to meet someone who wrote about angels from the basis of scripture. They laughed when I asked what "New Age" meant. Obviously, I did not live in California.

Heather began her talk with a description of Indian clothing. She pulled material for "Saris" and "Lungas" out of a dufflebag. For a long time she spoke about the villages, the culture and countryside.

As she began to speak about the people and tell their stories, tears came to her eyes and to those of us who listened. Heather described the poverty of a country where children are maimed in order to become better beggars. She described babies, bellies swollen to bursting, not from excessive food, but from malnutrition.

Heather told us how wives were chattels of

husbands and as such were beaten and bullied. She described days of hard labor in the fields for pennies as wages. This was not only normal in that culture, but an expected way of life.

Heather took the trip to India in complete faith that she would learn what she needed to learn to become a medical doctor there. She was to stay in a small village to serve in the local hospital as the doctor's assistant. When I asked how she had found the village where she was going, she said she called out (in English) the name of the village at the train station. As there was no response, she walked to the bus station and called out again, there.

Finally, a man approached her, bought her a ticket, put her on the right bus and disappeared. "Did I think he was an angel?, "Of course," I said. "Didn't you need a miracle? You were alone in a strange land where you could not speak the language, where you had purpose. Didn't you need a miracle?"

Heather told stories of sewage washing into the streets in a monsoon. She told stories of disease, infection and poverty. She explained the unsanitary and archaic conditions that Western culture would not understand. She told stories of how urgently medical aid and especially medical knowledge was needed in India.

Heather concluded her story with her never-ending love for the Indian people, her firm resolve to become a doctor to make a difference to the people of India. As fierce in her resolve as was Gandhi, we all admired her. She told us about the joy of the Indian people in nothingness and poverty. Heather said when she found India she found the harvesting place for her greatest purpose. I felt exactly the same way when I found the drug addictions and homeless in Santa Barbara, such a beautiful yet desolate place because of the extremes in wealth and in poverty.

Heather touched every heart that day at church. The love she had for her people created many healing miracles. The miracle revealed was a young college student coming back to Western culture, in our eyes, an angel, a healer, a transformed human. She had found her purpose.

What is yours?

THE NEED FOR MIRACLES

Miracles express God's intention of wholeness for society. It is this intervention of God in our lives that restores, heals and liberates humans to a place of dignity and power. The message of the miracle is that we are powerful beyond measure. Are we aware of our own powers? Do we act on them?

As we begin to acknowledge miracles in our lives we begin to acknowledge being stuck in our lives, remaining in any state that is restricting, constricting or limiting in any way. When we are clear about who we are, the energy that is around us and in us flows freely. We experience no strain. A feeling of happiness or peacefulness accompanies the miracles, that accompany those feelings. Isn't it magical when good things happen without effort? Was it a miracle of our

All people smile in the same language.

Proverbs 15:13~

own creation?

When we resist the energy of the universe or of our soul, pointing the way to greatness in our lives, we experience a shaky out-of-control feeling. The problem is that this feeling scares us. Truth is expressed in accepting these shaky feelings—feelings of insecurity or vulnerability as a sign that we are on the right track.

As we learn to embrace and move toward uncertainty with trust, miracles unfold in our lives.

Does it mean that travesties or tragedies are placed in our path in order to illuminate our power rather than to diminish it. Isn't that our greatest fear? In his 1994 inaugural speech, Nelson Mandela summed this up very well, with his words:

> *"Our deepest fear is not that we are inadequate.*
> *Our deepest fear is that we are powerful beyond measure.*
> *It is our light, not our darkness that frightens us "most.*
> *We ask ourselves, who am I to be brilliant, gorgeous, talented or famous?*
>
> *Actually, who are you not to be?*
> *You are a child of God.*
> *Your playing small doesn't serve the world.*
> *There is nothing enlightened about shrinking so that other people won't feel insecure around you.*

*We are born to make manifest the glory of God
that is within us.
It is not just in some of us; **it is in everyone.**
As we let our light shine, we unconsciously give
"other people permission to do the same.
As we are liberated from our own fear,
Our presence automatically liberates others."*

Fear is one of the most insidious and powerful prisoners of mankind. It is the feeling of impending doom or disaster in whatever we undertake that imprisons us. Like the Rock of Alcatraz, we become impenetrable until the walls of doubt come cascading, crumbling around us. Perhaps the greatest psychological debilitator of all time is the fear of success. We choose to be imprisoned by failure, by pain, by the frailties of our bodies, and repeat that imprisonment rather than to move out of our comfort zone to try something new in order to meet and greet success as we would an old friend.

Even a single hair casts a shadow.

Matthew 10:30~

People stay locked in careers they should not be in, locked in partnerships they should not be in, locked in marriages they should not be in, in order to remain in the stability of that state. To be out of control, to be out of balance, to be out of public expectation, causes such feelings of insecurity, guilt, physical harm, disease or death. When feelings of fear are ignored or defended against, they actually create a magnetism that draws the occurrence of the feared result into actuality. "Whatever you think about, you bring about." Has that ever happened to you? What you greatly feared has come upon you?

Recognition for the need for a miracle in your life begins with acknowledging a state of depression, dysfunction or disease as a sign for the need of change, and then embracing all the frightening emotions that take us in the direction of that change, and living our lives by going with the flow—or being in the flow, rather than using the change and the scary feelings as reasons for remaining in the "stuck" place.

It is reclaiming our own power, and the intensity and fullness of that power that should be directing us rather than remaining in a state of being half-comatose in our lifestyle and in our decisions. By choosing not to live life, take risks, do something new, have fun, we live half-deaths. Life gives us the tragedies to wake us up to the possibilities of enjoying each day, each hour, each minute, each second.

So what's stopping you from taking the risks you need to take in order to be fully alive? Why are you staying stuck? Is it easier to be stuck than to be afraid of what's really going on here?

We tend to live life as though we are hooked up to the intravenous bottle of doubt. Whenever a miracle arrives on our doorstep, we take another dose of doubt, Demerol, or some other current drug of numbness in order to remain in the old state. When we recognize fullness, freshness and reality of living the miracles in life, with glory and power this is so frightening that we stay addicted to half-deaths and half-truths.

Seek and you will find it. What is unsought will also go undetected.

Sophocles~

115

What are you denying about yourself that keeps coming up?

If you choose not to seek the truth of your own greatness, you will continue in stuck patterns that lead no-where. But you can be delivered from states of darkness by seeking the light of your own deliverance and embracing an alternative way. In the final analysis, it's the only way, as it embraces only truth.

Ask yourself:

Finding fault is life washing windows. The dirt is always on the other side.

Psalm 12:13~

- What is withholding the flow of energy and happiness in your life?
- To acknowledge your drug of choice and forgive yourself for taking it. Whatever it is, we all have addictions.
- To give recognition and acknowledgment to your fears, rather than dismissing them.
- Name ten major life goals and ten major accompanying fears that are imprisoning you. Break Free!

TRANSFORMATION OF THE UNIVERSE

Those of us who have experienced miracles see them as a liberating, enhancing, transforming intervention of God. Individuals liberated from illness and from diseases are restored not only to themselves, but to their relationships with others. They are enabled to begin life anew to choose new directions and new beginnings. Miracles urge us as humans not to base our lives on the security of physical determinism but on the mystery of God who creates and restores life. There is a higher power within us and outside of us that makes all things possible, and all miracles real.

Miracles, therefore, not only bring saving grace to your life, but transform and enhance your life as expressions of glory and light. Miracles inspire the unconquerable spirit of mankind to freedom and self-expression. Miracles speak to each of us in the very heart of our deepest longings. The fullness of the expression of the soul is characterized by transformation, not just the transformation of the individual soul but the transformation of all humanity in the liberation of its talents and inherent power. The transformation of the universe lies in the transformation of each individual soul, and the expression of that soul in its full potential. Are you expressing your full potential?

Miracles thus draw us toward the earth and at the same time detach us from it calling our senses out to play in order to provide a new direction for the spirit. Miracles preserve the tension between time and eternity.

This liberated spirit creates the new world order. It is the interplanetary light that dances between the stars to give us a glimpse of the future of undreamed wonders and raptures in recognizing and honoring the raptures in our life, we liberate the spirit of total freedom and the endless possibilities of unlimited power. It is play that liberates us.

Miracles, therefore, shed light on the

Clarity of purpose is communion with the soul. The voice inside becomes greater than the obstacles outside.

Angelica Wagner~

117

inauguration of the new world, a world of light and grace. This new world is a glimpse of the transformation that has begun in this current age. As we move into the new millennium, miracles will become commonplace. They will become daily occurrences to those who are aware of them, and who seek them.

The purpose in each of our lives is to awaken mankind to total service and total love. Miracles always occur as an expression of love. Love being the essence of all energy. Love is the unlimited power, infinite knowledge and absolute totality of all creative energy in its most perfect form. That is why the mystery of the miracle lies in messages of love toward each other and all humanity. Are you expressing love in order to create miracles?

If you're really ready for a miracle, learn to say "No" to those beliefs, actions and people that don't support your purpose. Learn to say "Yes" to the truth of your internal being, the God-Self within you. You are ready for a miracle when your spirit is free and happy. You will have embraced love as the answer to the transformation of your own divinity. The essence and power of your immortal soul will emerge in its magnificent glory.

Remember, you are the miracle!

Part Eight

Thoughts

CLOSING THOUGHTS

Scientists and geneticists have unlocked the incredible complexities of the body. In understanding cell functions they have discovered the infinitesimally minute particles of DNA called nucleotides. These nucleotides arrange themselves in complex combinations in each cell. There can be over three billion combinations in each microscopic cell in each part of our body.

Yet, each nucleotide arranges itself accurately in each cell as it divides in two, and the exact copy of DNA combinations is passed on to the next cell. As the cells multiply, they multiply exactly time after time with less than one in a billion chance of an error of that cell mutating or dying.

If each microorganism in our body, each tiny cell intrinsically knows how to differentiate into blood, bone or organ, why don't we listen to our cells ? No one has yet unlocked the secret of cell differentiation. Could this be a miracle? If our cells intrinsically know what to do in order to be their very best, why is it so difficult for our bodies to form partnerships with our minds, hearts and spirits to catapult our lives forward?

Is the miracle found in listening to the voice of pain in our bodies or learning to open our hearts in understanding? Accepting the healing which is often fully given with love, and actively seeking the signs and actions of love that are frequently given, (often rejected) are the beginnings of miracles.

You have been sent to the world to enrich its capacity for growth. You are here for a reason. Discover your life purpose and break through those barriers of human confinement to choose your new world.

Create your own miracles!

Move forward to receive in peace and love.

Allow yourself the luxury of greatness in your life!!

Remember, YOU are the miracle!

BIBLIOGRAPHY

Acquinas; St. Thomas; *Treatise on the Separate Substances*, trans. by F. J. Lescoe(West Hartford, 1959)

Anon; *The book of Enoch*, trans. by R. H. Charles (London 1917)

J.B.Aufhuser; *The Miracles of Jesus* trans. A. Wimmer(Notre Dame1968) Shannon, Ireland

J. B. Aufhauser; *Antike Jesusgezeugnisse* (1925) cited in Messner

Baker; *The Encyclopedia of the Bible Volume I*, Edited by Walter Elwell (Baker Book House, Grand Rapids , Michigan

R. Bultman; *The Question of Wonder in Faith and Understanding*, (New York,1969)

Burnham, Sophy; *A Book of Angels* (Ballantine Books, New York)

Charelsworth; James; *Old Testament Pseudipigrapha Volume One* (Doubleday 1983, new York)

Corbin, Henry; *Avicenna and the Visionary Recital*, trans. by W. R.. Trask (London 1960)

Daniel, Orville; *A Harmony of the Four Gospels*, International Version

Eliade, Mircea; *Shamanism; Archaic Techniques of Ecstacy*, trans. by W. R. Trask

Howard Loxton; *The Art of the Angels;* Oriental Press (Dubai)

Kerenyi, Carl; *The Gods of the Greeks* (Harmondsworth, 1958)

Latourelle; *The Miracle of Jesus* (Paulist Press, New York)

Nasr, Seyyad Hossein; *An Introduction to Islamic Cosmological Doctrines* (Cambridge, Mass)

Plato; *Phaedrus and Letters VII and VIII*, trans. by W. Hamelton

R. Reitzenstein; *Helenistische Wunderzahlung* (Leipzig,1906)

Saso, Michael; *The teachings of the Taoist Masters*, (New Haven, London 1978)

Shaya, Leo; *The Universal Meaning of the Kabbalah*

Swindoll; *Flying closer to the Flame*, (Word Incorporated, Dallas, Texas 1993)

The Symposium; trans. by W. Hamilton (Harmsworth 1951)

Ward, Bernard; *Angels* (Globe Communications 1995 Boca Raton)

Williamson, Marianne; *Illuminata , A Return To Prayer* (Berkley, Publishing Group 1994)

Zondervan; *The New Layman's Parallel Bible* (Zondervan, Grand rapids Michigan)

Change has ALWAYS brought opportunity for those who have the courage to act.

Many of those who have purchased "Secrets of Success" have already achieved their desired goals with outstanding and extraordinary results . . . for them, business is booming!

Let me help you turn fear into courage as you apply the principles of proven success. Why not start now, and watch your business take off! Since you are already doing what you love to do, "Secrets of Success in Real Estate Excellence" will only further inspire you to do it in the BEST ways possible.

Make the choice NOW for your future.

Yours with Success,

Angie Wagner

ORDER FORM ————————————————————————

Name:_____

Address: _____

City: _____

Province/State: _____   Postal/Zip Code: _____

Phone Number: _____   Facsimile Number: _____

		METHOD OF PAYMENT
Secrets of Success Workbook	$29.95	
Secrets of Success Tapes Series		
(East)	$159.00	☐ Cheque enclosed
(West)	$159.00	☐ Mastercard / Visa
Courage Tape	$10.00	
Purchase any one tape and book	$179.00	
Purchase any two tapes and book	$300.00	Credit Card Number:
SUBTOTAL _____		
GST _____		Expiry Date
PST _____		Signature
TOTAL _____		

MAIL TO: **DREAMAKERS INTERNATIONAL INC.,**
6850 Millcreek Drive, Mississauga ON   L5N 4J9
Telephone: (905) 858-3434
Facsimile: (905) 858-2682

Are YOU ready for a Miracle with Chiropractic?

Chiropractic is leading the way in the paradigm shift towards whole health. The principled chiropractors and the patients they serve share the same passion for chiropractic, the same love for the healing.

My book "Are You Ready for a Miracle with Chiropractic," is finally being published and ready for sale to your practices and your region. Thank you for all the wonderful stories you contributed.

Yours with Success,

Angie Wagner

ORDER FORM ——————————————————————————

Name: _____

Address: _____

City: _____

Province/State: _____ Postal/Zip Code: _____

Phone Number: _____ Facsimile Number: _____

Dedication if you wish
book(s) personally
inscribed:

Number of Copies	Unit Price	Quantity	Total Amt of Order	Add 7% G.S.T.	Add Shipping Charge	Total Payable
25 or more	$8.00 ea.				$10.00	
10 to 24	$10.00 ea.				$5.00	
1 to 9	$12.00 ea.				$2.00	

"CREATING THE PRACTICE OF YOUR DREAMS"

Book (CA's) $29.95   No.____ Total _____ G.S.T. _____ Total_____ Payable_____

3 Audio Tapes (CA's) $59.95 No.____ Total _____ G.S.T. _____ Total_____ Payable_____

METHOD OF PAYMENT

☐ Cash
☐ Cheque enclosed
☐ Mastercard / Visa

Credit Card # _____

Expiry Date _____

Signature   _____

MAIL TO: **DREAMAKERS INTERNATIONAL INC.,**
              6850 Millcreek Drive, Mississauga ON   L5N 4J9

Telephone: (905) 858-3434
Facsimile: (905) 858-2682

An extensive library of Angelica Wagner's ongoing live lectures are available on audio and visual cassette and may be ordered by calling

USA: 1-800- 860-8187 EXT. 6226

Canada: 1-800-927-8139 EXT. 6226.

If this book has not touched your heart,

or changed your life in some way,

please do not hesitate to return it for a refund.

NOTES